KT-362-124

TRACING YOUR ANCESTORS

A Guide for Family Historians

SIMON FOWLER

Pen & Sword
FAMILY HISTORY

First published in Great Britain in 2011 by
PEN AND SWORD FAMILY HISTORY
an imprint of
Pen & Sword Books Ltd
47 Church Street
Barnsley
South Yorkshire
S70 2AS

Copyright © Simon Fowler 2011

ISBN 978 1 84415 948 2

The right of Simon Fowler to be identified as Author of this Work
has been asserted by him in accordance with the Copyright, Designs
and Patents Act 1988.

A CIP catalogue record for this book is
available from the British Library.

All rights reserved. No part of this book may be reproduced or
transmitted in any form or by any means, electronic or mechanical
including photocopying, recording or by any information storage and
retrieval system, without permission from the Publisher in writing.

Typeset in 10pt Palatino by Mac Style, Beverley, East Yorkshire
Printed and bound in India by Replika Press Pvt. Ltd.

Pen & Sword Books Ltd incorporates the Imprints of Pen & Sword
Aviation, Pen & Sword Maritime, Pen & Sword Military,
Wharncliffe Local History, Pen and Sword Select, Pen and Sword
Military Classics, Leo Cooper, Remember When, Seaforth Publishing
and Frontline Publishing.

For a complete list of Pen & Sword titles please contact
PEN & SWORD BOOKS LIMITED
47 Church Street, Barnsley, South Yorkshire, S70 2AS, England
E-mail: enquiries@pen-and-sword.co.uk
Website: www.pen-and-sword.co.uk

TRACING YOUR
ANCESTORS

C014772946

FAMILY HISTORY FROM PEN & SWORD BOOKS

Tracing Your Yorkshire Ancestors
Rachel Bellerby

Tracing Your Royal Marine Ancestors
Richard Brooks and Matthew Little

Tracing Your Pauper Ancestors
Robert Burlison

Tracing Your Labour Movement Ancestors
Mark Crail

Tracing Your Army Ancestors
Simon Fowler

A Guide to Military History on the Internet
Simon Fowler

Tracing Your Northern Ancestors
Keith Gregson

Your Irish Ancestors
Ian Maxwell

Tracing Your Scottish Ancestors
Ian Maxwell

Tracing Your London Ancestors
Jonathan Oates

Tracing Your Air Force Ancestors
Phil Tomaselli

Tracing Your Secret Service Ancestors
Phil Tomaselli

Tracing Your Criminal Ancestors
Stephen Wade

Tracing Your Police Ancestors
Stephen Wade

Tracing Your Jewish Ancestors
Rosemary Wenzerul

Fishing and Fishermen
Martin Wilcox

CONTENTS

ACKNOWLEDGEMENTS

I am grateful to the support and encouragement shown by the team at Pen & Sword over many years, particularly Rupert Harding and Brian Elliott. My wife Sylvia has also been very encouraging and we'll meet some of her ancestors in these pages. Readers and writers on both *Family History Monthly* and *Ancestors Magazine* over the past decade have challenged my assumptions and asked difficult questions – which I hope I have answered. Lastly, this book is for my long lost cousin Jennifer Thornton. She bought a copy of *Joys of Family History* and contacted me after spotting similarities with my family tree. It turns out we are cousins. We have shared our research and have become friends. So it proves that some good comes from writing books like these!

Word of warning

Nothing stands still any longer in the world of family history. The information contained in this book is correct at the date of writing, that is November 2010. However, addresses do change, websites come and go, prices go up (rarely down), and new services come online, so it is important to check where possible. I have tried to future proof the book by including details of projects which are likely to come to fruition over the next couple of years. But inevitably there are others which I do not know about.

Fortunately the various genealogical magazines will keep you informed of new websites, services and resources. And online, Dick Eastman's and Chris Paton's genealogical blogs are pretty good in carrying the latest news: http://blog.eogn.com and http://scottishancestry.blogspot.com

PREFACE

For nearly four decades family history – genealogy – has been one of the fastest growing hobbies in Britain. Looking for one's ancestors is now an incredibly popular pastime – perhaps a million people in Britain are engaged in the search, and another five million say that they would like to take up the hobby. Genealogy is the third most popular subject on the internet and data providers such as Ancestry and Findmypast are one of the few online businesses that make large profits.

You can be any age, creed, shape or size to start tracing your ancestors, although it is true to say that most researchers are retired or semi-retired. All you need to begin is an enquiring mind, a notebook and a sharp pencil. And having a computer and basic skills using the internet are now almost essential as well.

Family history is something that you can pick up or put down when it suits you. After all your ancestors are not going to disappear. How you tackle your research is up to you. There is no pressure to trace everybody you are descended from. Indeed, as you will discover it is nearly impossible to tick them all off. Most people end up only researching one side of their family or a few ancestors who particularly interest them. Others stop their research at the beginning of the nineteenth century, which is about when the records become more difficult to use (but rather more interesting).

There are just enough challenges and puzzles to solve to make tracing your ancestors stimulating and there is nothing quite like the buzz you will get when you finally managed to track down that elusive great-grandmother. And if one forebear seems to appear from nowhere and irritatingly disappears into the ether a few years later, well, there are plenty of other ancestors out there for you to find.

One of the great things about the pastime is how friendly and helpful most family historians are. If you become confused on your first visit to The National Archives or your local history library, the chance is that your neighbour at the microfilm reader will be only too pleased to point you in the right direction (actually stopping them without hurting their feelings can be a problem!). Genealogists are very sociable as you will find if you join a local family history society or beginners course at the adult education centre.

For some people family history leads them into totally new directions. A friend of mine has become the world expert in William Cuffey – the nineteenth-century black radical leader. While another has spent years tracing the ancestry of the Brontë sisters – they proved to be rather more interesting than her own family! Does it matter? No it doesn't!

This book was intended as an update of *Joys of Family History* which I wrote for The National Archives, then the Public Record Office over ten years ago. However, the genealogical world and, in particular, the resources that we use in our research has changed almost beyond recognition over the past decade that almost nothing of the original text remains.

In particular the internet was then becoming increasingly important but nobody saw the impact it would have on family history. In this book I have assumed that you are online at home (or have an understanding employer) and that you are familiar with the basics of using the internet. If not, your local library may be able to help. So much is now available online it would be churlish to ignore these resources.

Frankly, what you do and how you do it is up to you. Other genealogical guides tend to be more structured, but most researchers seem to pick and choose as they see fit.

However, before you start you need to be aware of a few principles.

You should always work from what you already know, and what you can prove. If you don't you will end up with what Michael Gandy, one of Britain's top genealogists, calls a file marked "ancestors I used to have". Oh, and never assume. If you assume something because you have not found any evidence, remember that it is only a guess, and is likely to be wrong.

Now get out there and start tracing your family – be prepared to be surprised and delighted! But beware the sad fare of Cousin Kay:

> There's been a change in Cousin Kay,
> We've noticed as of late.
> She's always reading history, or jotting down some date.
> She's tracing back the family, we all have pedigrees.
> Kay's got a hobby –
> She's climbing Family Trees.
> Poor Malcolm does the cooking and now, or so he states,
> He even has to wash the cups and even dinner plates!

Well, Kay cannot be bothered,
She's busy as can be
Compiling genealogy for the Family Tree.
She has no time to dog-sit, the living room's a fright,
No buttons left on Malcolm's shirt,
(Tho' the garden looks all right).
She's given up her drawing and the serials on TV –
The only thing she does these days
Is climb the Family Tree.
To some it's just a hobby, but to Kay it's so much more.
She learns the joys and heartaches
Of those who've gone before.
They loved, they lost, they laughed, they cried and now for all to see
They live again, in spirit,
Around the Family Tree!
(Anon)

My great-grandmother Philippa Crozier with three of her children photographed in the early 1890s. Adrian Lead

Chapter 1

STARTING AT HOME

Family history is like a jigsaw puzzle. There's lots of pieces which may (or indeed may not) fit together to build a picture of where you come from and your ancestors lives. But you have to start somewhere, open the box and spread the pieces on the table so to speak. And the only place you can do this is at home.

Start by thinking about what you know already. Naturally the more information you have to start off with, the better it is – but if you know next to nothing, there's no need to panic. I have had students from both extremes who have literally just known the birthdates of their parents (in one case a student only knew about her mother), while others, like my cousin, has papers, photographs and artefacts going back to the eighteenth century, including one very fearsome portrait of a matriarch whose eyes disapprovingly follow you around the room.

Family history guides sometimes tell you to start by talking to the oldest members of the family. This is certainly sound advice if you are young, but most researchers find that they are the oldest in their families: as people tend to develop an interest in where they came from late in life. It's a common lament that 'I wish I had asked granny when she was still alive.' But of course you can't – you have to work with what you've got.

But if you do have elderly relatives it is well worth talking to them about what they remember about their parents and grandparents as well as discussing family legends and stories. They can often remember back before the Second World War and possibly can recount events that happened many years before they were born. It is preferable to see them in person, rather than write or telephone. A suggested set of questions is on page 175.

Don't necessarily believe what they will tell you; always check it. There is however often a grain of truth in family tradition. In particular oral history researchers have found that interviewees have a tendency to imagine that they were present at great events – such as the Coronation or the D-Day landings – either because they remember seeing newsreels or TV programmes about them or conflate several different events. Just because Uncle Fred was in the Army during the Second World War it does not mean he stormed the Normandy beaches, but could have seen the war out as a stores clerk at Catterick.

Second World War Dorset soldiers aboard their landing craft on the run-in to Gold Beach during the D-Day Landing. Pen & Sword Books Ltd

If you have them it is a good idea to take photographs with you to refresh the memory. People like to look at pictures and can often supply names for unknown individuals in a family snapshot.

But don't try to do too much at one time, as the elderly can tire easily. And for heaven's sake be tactful and understanding of the interviewee's feelings, so don't barge in and demand papers, names and so on. Accept that not everybody is as enthusiastic as you are about the family. And of course some people, for whatever reason, don't want to be interviewed, or they may have painful memories which they won't want to discuss with you. Even so you might find some real pointers to your family's past which you may never come across otherwise.

Everybody has interesting memories and when they go they take them with them. Once you have written up your relatives' stories you could consider donating yours to an online oral history resource, such as the Nations' Memory Bank at www.nationsmemorybank.com, or a regional equivalent.

Most families have a collection of heirlooms. Of course they do vary tremendously, but they are good place to start for they may tell you something about your immediate ancestors. If you can't find very much, other members

---

WHAT TO ASK

Work out simple questions before hand: how..., who..., why..., when... and then...; or use a ready prepared questionnaire. This may be restrictive – but you won't forget anything. On the other hand don't stick to it rigidly, for you may miss some interesting stories
Here are some questions you should think about asking:

- What is your name?
- Do you have any nicknames by which you are, or were, known?
- When and where were you born?
- When and where did you get married? (How many people came to your wedding?)
- How many children do you have and when were they born?
- What did you do for an occupation? (What was your favourite job?)
- What is your earliest memory?
- When and where was your favourite holiday?
- Who were your parents?
- When and where were they born?
- When and where did they get married?
- When and where did they die?
- What was the most remarkable thing about your father?
- What did he do for a living?
- Describe him – was he tall or short, fat or thin?
- What was the most remarkable thing about your mother?
- What did she do for a living?
- Describe her – was she tall or short, fat or thin?
- Do you have any brothers and sisters, and who are they?
- When were they born?
- When did they marry?
- When did they die?
- What did they do for a living?

A collection of family papers. Margaret G Powling

of the family may be able to help. And it's always worth asking around. Several times before his death my father produced large envelopes full of goodies, which contained papers and photographs about ancestors going back 150 years – although I am still not clear who is always linked to whom.

The sort of things you might find are:

• Photographs and photograph albums (see below)
• Letters and diaries. They can be often quite poignant. I always regret that when my grandmother died, the last – unopened – letters from her favourite brother, killed in the last days of the First World War, were thrown away
• Official papers, from birth and marriage certificates to National Identity Cards and call-up papers
• Press cuttings – usually of course about family members. My father's papers contain funeral notices for the Rev George Paul Belcher and his wife who died in the 1880s. I have recently found he is my great-great-grandfather, after whom his grandson Paul Belcher Fowler was named

My nephew examines the telescope presented to my great-great-grandfather John Fowler in 1859. The Author

- Family bibles – may list births, christenings, marriages and deaths. If you're very lucky the information may go back centuries
- Artefacts. Silver, and portraits, in particular are often passed down and may be inscribed. Wedding dresses and christening clothes are other items which may pass between the generations. In particular look to see whether there are any inscriptions. I have an old telescope which was presented to my 5xgrandfather John Fowler in 1859 by the grateful passengers of the *Normahal* for saving their lives during a storm. There are several passenger lists online for the ship suggesting that it was an emigrant ship to Australia

A letter from the front written to my great-aunt Bijou by my great-uncle Stanley Crozier.
Adrian Lead

Identifying old photographs

Most families have got collections of photographs showing our ancestors at various stages in their lives, as well as family groups, special events such as a wedding or christening, and snaps of the area in which people lived or went on holiday too, perhaps showing bomb damage or a royal visit. In short the sort of pictures we still take today.

The earliest photographs date from 1840s, although in practice few families have any before the 1860s. Almost immediately, they became immensely popular. Specialist photographic studios sprang up around the country taking people's portraits. Slow exposure times meant that it was difficult to take shots without the subjects moving, which is why most early pictures look very posed.

The 1890s saw the first proper hand-held cameras, such as Kodak's Box Brownie, which were cheap enough to allow millions of people to take up the hobby. Picture postcards also became very popular. Colour film generally became commonly used after the Second World War. And over the past decade old-fashioned film has largely been replaced by digital images.

With luck the photographs are safely captioned in albums or have the names of the sitter written on the back. But in practice this rarely happens. After all if you took the photograph you know who the people you photographed are so you don't need to note down who they are. When my mother left Germany before the Second World War as a teenager, she took a photograph album with carefully mounted pictures of her family. Each photograph is carefully labelled, with captions such as "Fritz und Otto". But I only found the album after her death, so now it will be a Herculean task to find out who these people were and their relationship to my mother.

So make it easy for your family in the future – caption each photo with details of who the individuals are and when and where the photograph was taken.

That said, photographs can give clues that might help you identify individuals or tell you something about their lives.

Cartes de visites in particular usually include details of the photographic studio either on the front or more often on the back of the photograph. With rare exceptions the studios have long closed and any records lost. But you may be able to identify when the studio was in operation from a trade directory. There are also several directories of old photographers. An online one for London is at www.photolondon.org.uk and less detailed information can be found at www.cartedevisite.co.uk. Others for Sussex is at www.photohistory-sussex.co.uk, and East Anglia www.early-photographers.org.uk; and no doubt there are also websites for other localities.

The background in the photo may also provide clues, particular if the photograph was taken somewhere easily identifiable like Blackpool beach or at a national event such as the Festival of Britain in 1951. Staff at the appropriate local studies library may be able to help.

In many ways the easiest way at least to date a photograph is through the clothes people wear. Then as now fashions changed regularly, particularly

A page from my mother's photograph album. Who Dora, Heinz and Jochem will almost certainly never be known. The Author

for women, so it may be possible to use the vanity of the sitter to your own benefit! But there are problems with this approach – firstly older people and men tended to not be so up to date as their daughters and sisters, and in addition poorer families were unable to keep up with the fashions in the way that their richer cousins could.

Clothes were also a powerful indicator of social class. The shabbier the clothes and the cheaper the cut then generally the poorer the sitter. A century ago an American journalist, Jack London, decided to explore the East End. After buying a set of workmen's clothes from a second-hand store he noted: "In crossing crowded thoroughfares I found I had to be, if anything, more lively in avoiding vehicles, and it was strikingly impressed upon me that my

A cartes de visite taken of a young lady by J H Blomfield & Co of Hastings in the 1890s. Sussex Photo History

life had cheapened in direct ratio to my clothes. When before I inquired the way of a policeman, I was usually asked, 'Bus or 'ansom [Hansom Cab], sir?' But now the query became, 'Walk or ride?'"

You may be able to guess an approximate age. However, people in general before the Second World War aged much earlier, so by today's standards even fairly young people can look old. Again this does vary by class – the poorer your ancestors were the older they may look.

Jayne Shrimpton, *Family Photographs and how to date them* (Countryside Books, 2007) is a good introduction. There are also various websites that can help, although most are American and you should be aware that American clothing was rather different to that worn in Britain. Two excellent British websites which may be able to help are www.cartedevisite.co.uk and www.cartes.freeuk.com/time/date.htm.

IDENTIFYING MILITARY UNIFORMS

Many families have photographs of men in Army uniform, particularly from the two world wars. With some effort and a bit of luck you should be able to find more about the man and his service from looking carefully at the picture, although beware this can be a minefield which trips up even specialists.

The first thing to do is to try to identify his regiment from a cap badge or belt buckle. Chevrons high up on the sleeve would indicate that he was a non-commissioned officer – while others low down on the sleeve indicate the award of good conduct medals or years served overseas, while other patches might denote the number of times he was wounded, and the division to which his unit belonged. Over his heart should be the medal ribbons, or possibly the medals themselves. Pips on his shoulder, a smarter cut of uniform and possibly a Sam Browne leather belt would suggest that the sitter is an officer.

Studio photograph of a soldier in the Yorks & Lancs Regiment, taken in Rotherham, in 1917. Andrew Featherstone

Naturally the Navy and the RAF did their own thing. The best introduction to the subject is Neil Storey, *Military Photographs and How to Identify Them* (Countryside Books, 2009). An excellent guide to First World War Army uniforms is at www.4thgordons.com/I-Spybook%20of%20 Uniforms1.2.pdf. For the Navy in the twentieth century there is www.sea yourhistory.org.uk and the eccentric www.godfreydykes.info but neither is very satisfactory.

Looking after family heirlooms

With a little care your heirlooms can be kept safe for future generations to enjoy. However, you should always seek professional advice about items in poor condition. In particular you need to guard against the five perils of:

- Heat – constantly warm temperatures are very bad, particularly for paper as it will dry out and become brittle
- Water – water from leaky pipes and damp rooms are a great threat to heirlooms. In particular paper can absorb large amounts of water in damp conditions and can buckle or the ink can run
- Light – is a particular problem for it causes fading. Direct sunlight is the most harmful form. Do not place valuable photographs and paintings on walls or mantelpieces, especially where sunlight can get at them. Why not display reproductions instead?
- Growth – mould is a particular menace, it can grow when items have been left in damp conditions. If you find evidence of this seek professional advice
- People – old documents and photographs do not like being handled, so why not get copies made and take these on your research trips? Pick documents and photographs up from the edge to prevent passing potentially damaging grease from your fingers to the document or surface of the photograph

Your family heirlooms should be kept in a cool, dark and dry place. My papers are under the bed in the north-facing spare-room. It is also a good idea to store them in tight-fitting boxes as added protection against light and damp. Shoe boxes will do, at least as a start, but the cardboard contains dangerous acids which will ultimately damage paper stored in this way. Try to place individual documents and photographs so that they do not become folded. And please do not use sticky tape to mend damaged documents, as over time the tape will become brittle and permanently mark the document.

If you want to know more the Institute of Conservation has published a series of useful guides to preserving and caring for family papers – www.icon.org.uk. And if you want to preserve your papers it is worth considering buying archival boxes and paper to store them in. Waterman is an excellent company with a range of different boxes and related products and they should be able to help, so try www.watermanswebworld.com.

A collection of family papers which should be cared for so that future generations can enjoy them. The Author

Be organised

One of the most important decisions you will make could be taken without any real thought – how to keep the information that you have in a way which is safe and which you can easily use. For as you progress you will accumulate a large amount of paperwork – certificates, photographs and the like. And as I have discovered to my cost, unless you keep all this safe and sound you will spend hours and hours looking for that elusive slip of paper. Oh, and don't write notes on the backs of envelopes because inevitably you will lose them.

The best way is to keep a folder for each individual ancestor where you can store items about them. On the cover, or on a covering sheet, you could

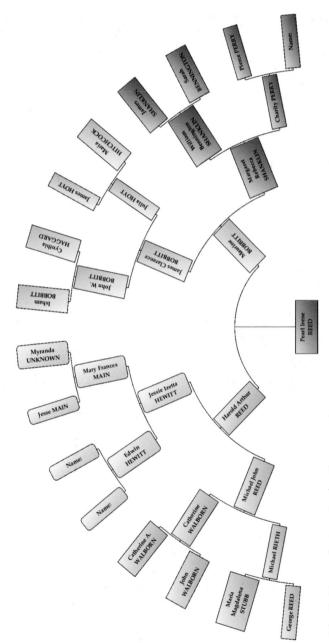

A family history chart. Author's collection

write their dates of birth, marriage and death and their relationship to you and other information such as: name(s) of wife/husband, the dates of their birth/death; children (with dates of birth, marriage and death); occupation; military service (if yes, provide brief details of unit and dates in the service); addresses where they lived.

It can be helpful to maintain an ancestral chart or family tree for each branch of your family where you can record brief details about each member. I've included one on page 187.

In the long term you may wish to buy software to help keep track of their research and draw up family trees. And of course anything which encourages you to be methodical and organised is to be encouraged!

Genealogy software will provide you with comprehensive reports and charts so you can organise and see the progress of your research. Some of these reports and charts include:

- Ancestor charts include a person's direct-line ancestors, so you can see exactly how far back a line goes
- Ancestral narrative reports are book-style reports that begin with a specific person and follow that person's lineage like a story. This is a great way to share your research with family members and friends
- Family charts show entire families including husband, wife and children

Genealogy software include tons of easy-to-use tools that will help you discover and organise your research. Organisational tools can link people together based on relationships, merge individuals into family trees, help spot problems and locate duplicate entries. Selecting the right genealogical software program may make all the difference in how much satisfaction and information you will derive from your research. Accessing, recording and reviewing data should be easy, as well as fun.

You also need to consider these facilities:

- Ease of use. One of the most important features in genealogy software is its user-friendliness, meaning it's easy for beginners and experienced computer users alike. The program should be well organised and easy to navigate
- Ease of installation and setup. The software should be straightforward and simple to install and setup on your computer, without any errors or confusing steps

- Features. Genealogy software should include all of the features necessary to research and organise your family tree including reports charts, searching capabilities, web access and insightful ways to store data
- Help and documentation. The genealogy software developer should provide ample help in the form of FAQs, email and phone support, online course and product tutorials so anyone can learn to use the program and conveniently access customer support
- British editions. Most programs are designed for use by American genealogists and many not always be suitable or easily adaptable by their British cousins. Try to buy a British edition or British software

Example of family history software. Family Historian

The best-selling software is Family Tree Maker published by Ancestry. It is widely avaible and most reviewers think favourably of it, and there is a British edition. Find more at www.familytreemaker.com. The best piece of

---

"PURE ANGLO-SAXON WITH JUST A DASH OF VIKING"

This was how Tony Hancock described his heritage in *The Blood Donor*. Through DNA testing surely we can now find exactly where we came from. The answer is up to a point. And although DNA testing can be a help, in certain circumstances the cheap tests now generally available are basically a waste of time and money. In *Ancestors Magazine* the deputy editor tested three different companies and came up with three different results – one of which said she had Chinese ancestry. So far as anybody knew her ancestors had never been further east than Frinton! Basically the more markers that are tested then the more useful the results will be. Tests vary in price between £89 and £400 depending on the numbers of markers examined. Personally I wouldn't bother. However, if you want to find out more then the best introduction is Chris Pomery's *Family History in the Genes* (The National Archives, 2007).

software purely designed for British users is the well-regarded Family Historian – details at www.family-historian.co.uk. For Mac users there is the excellent Reunion, see www.leisterpro.com.

There are comparative reviews of most software at http://genealogy-software-review.toptenreviews.com. In addition most of the family history magazines publish reviews of the latest software.

Chapter 2

FINDING INFORMATION ONLINE

Once you have built up a basic family tree from talking to your relatives and family papers you will need to turn to resources online and at archives and libraries (see next chapter).

It is now almost impossible to conduct your family history without resource to the internet. But why should you, when the online resources are generally easier to use, certainly many times quicker to find what you want, and allows you to find links between families and individuals which otherwise might have remained hidden.

However, the downside is that the indexing of names can on occasion leave something to be desired and it can sometimes be difficult to manipulate the databases to turn up any reference to your ancestor. So although your ancestor may be in the records they either don't appear in the index or more likely have had their name misspelt by the indexer. Errors like this happen less frequently than they used to, but they still occur.

Resources online

People may tell you that everything about your ancestors is on the internet and all it takes is an evening sat in front of a computer to be able to trace your family back to Adam and Eve. Well, this is true at least up to a point. There is a huge amount available and more added every day.

Websites can split simply into two – those which charge for information and those which are free. As you will see you can get a surprising amount for free, but in general you will need to subscribe to one or two services.

The two big companies are:

- Ancestry – www.ancestry.co.uk
- Findmypast – www.findmypast.com

Both offer a variety of subscription packages. Roughly, however, the more you pay the more you get. It is worth looking out for special offers. Both sometimes offer 14-day free access, while Findmypast occasionally offers discounts on subscriptions packages.

WHAT WWW.ANCESTRY.CO.UK OFFERS

The major resources on their website:

- English, Welsh and some Scottish censuses 1841–1901 (and 1911 is likely to be added in due course)
- Birth, marriage and death indexes
- Army service records and medal index cards of the First World War
- Incoming passenger lists 1878–1960
- Parish and other records for London
- Access to databases on other Ancestry websites worldwide
- Indexes to wills 1858–1946

There are lots of smaller databases as well.

In conclusion
In favour
- More resources than its rivals
- 14-day free trial
- Good birth, marriage and death indexes

Against
- The search engine can be hard to use (and in general it is not always easy to find your way around)
- Reputation for poor indexing
- Often they have only included part of a collection and it is not always clear what is already available and what has to be added

WHAT WWW.FINDMYPAST.CO.UK OFFERS

The major resources on their website are:

- English and Welsh censuses 1841–1911
- Outward passenger lists 1890–1960
- Birth, marriage and death indexes
- Pre-1914 soldiers' papers

There are also a number of smaller databases, including access to parts of the National Burial Index.

In conclusion

In favour
- Well designed website
- Useful e-newsletter
- Unique access to 1911 census

Against
- Fewer resources than Ancestry
- Irritating and distracting banner advertisements

Other commercial websites

There are other – smaller – sites which may be worth looking at. These can divided between those which roughly duplicate the material held by Ancestry and Findmypast, and those which have unique material. If you are just looking for the basic resources they can be cheaper than the 'big boys' and their indexes may well be better.

Each has all or part of the census, birth, marriage and death indexes and scans of a variety of old books and directories:

- Family relatives – www.familyrelatives.com
- The Genealogist – www.thegenealogist.co.uk (also has pre-1837 non-conformist birth, marriage and death registers)
- Genes Reunited – www.genesreunited.com (this site is likely to disappear as it has been bought by Findmypast)

Unique material
- Documents Online – www.nationalarchives.gov.uk/documentsonline
  Pre-1858 wills; naval and RAF service records pre-1920, merchant seamen records; WW1 medal index cards. Unusually you pay for each image downloaded rather than buy a subscription to the whole of the website. Downloads are currently £3.50 each (£2 for medal index cards)
- Origins network – www.origins.net
  Pre-1837 records
- The Original Record – www.theoriginalrecord.com
  Extracts from thousands of records arranged by surname
- ScotlandsPeople – www.scotlandspeople.gov.uk
  Resources for researching Scottish ancestry including birth, marriage and death records from the sixteenth century and census returns 1841–1901

Resources for free

There are getting on for 300,000 websites devoted to family history, although most just contain family trees which are only of interest to the immediate family. I have mentioned the best where appropriate in this book, but here are a few general sites which are worth exploring.

Gateway sites
- Cyndi's list – www.cyndislist.com
  Has links to 265,000 genealogy websites worldwide. The site is simply arranged by subject or country so it is fairly easy to find what you want.
- Price and Co – http://pricegen.com/english_genealogy.htm
  Links to the top 500 British websites

Miscellaneous data and indexes

- Ancestral Information – www.ancestor-search.info
  There are many, many sites for family history beginners (not that you need to visit them now you have this book), but I particularly like this one for its clear lay out and simple guidance to the major sources. It is also up to date
- GENUKI – www.genuki.org.uk
  Information about the United Kingdom and Ireland arranged by county and nation
- UK Genealogical Data – www.ukgdl.org.uk
  Links to nearly 1100 websites with databases and other resources
- Vision of Britain – www.visionofbritain.org.uk
  Has much about British history including accounts of Britain through the ages by travel writers, digitised copies of early Ordnance Survey maps and pages on landscape history. Also of use in a similar vein is www.british-history.ac.uk
- Wikipedia – http://en.wikipedia.org
  The greatest encyclopaedia online with particularly good sections on British military history. It should be able to answer most questions. The National Archives has its own wiki at http://yourarchives.nationalarchives.gov.uk and a wiki specifically for genealogy is at www.eogen.com

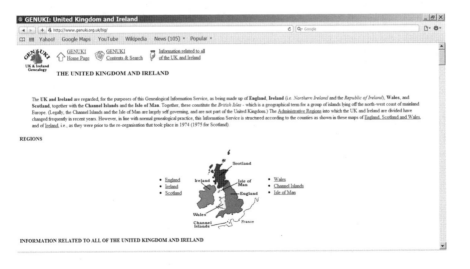

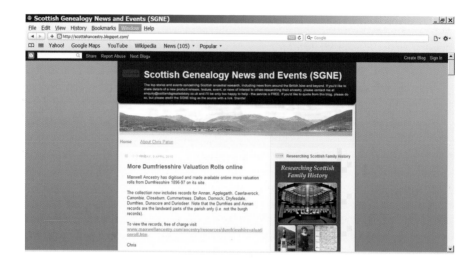

Websites may not be much help in providing answers to particular problems once you start researching an individual ancestor. An alternative is the various online discussion forums which are ideal places to ask questions or learn from the experience of others. I belong for example to a First World War mailing list which has a constant stream of requests for help with members' research which are patiently answered by other list members. In addition there are snippets of news and debates on various related topics: a recent one was how it was possible to enlist under a false name!

The best list of mailing lists is at www.genuki.org.uk/wg. For details of those specifically relevant to the British Isles, see www.genuki.org.uk/indexes/ MailingLists.html. Indeed this page lists almost all genealogical mailing lists, so there are also links to lists for particular surnames, places or occupations.

There are various blogs where you can catch up with the latest news from the family history world. The two best are Chris Paton's http://scottishancestry. blogspot.com and Dick Eastman's http://blog.eogn.com.

Placing family data online
Many genealogy programs and data providers allow you to place information about your ancestors online. This allows you to share information with

cousins and other relatives around the world. However, you need to be careful putting up details of people who are still living in order to protect them from fraudsters and scammers.

There are several websites that will also put up details for you, the best known of which is Genes Reunited (www.genesreunited.co.uk). Unfortunately although there are hundreds of millions of names to be found here it can be very hard to find the tree or relatives that you want. However, it is likely that the site's new owner, Findmypast, will improve matters.

LESS IS MORE

It can be infuriatingly difficult to find individuals in commercial website search engines. Paradoxically the rule often is to type in fewer details rather than more. Often the name – Paul Belcher and possibly a county of residence or birth, such as Kent or Leicestershire – will be enough, even so you might have to scroll through several screens to find the entry you want.

USING GOOGLE

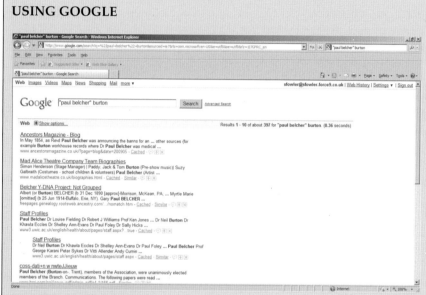

Page from www.google.com

If you are like most people you've probably typed your name into Google to see whether you appear online. You can of course do the same for your ancestors – you might be surprised what you might find. Of course it helps if they were reasonably well to do, but even if they came from a long line of agricultural labourers it is worth giving it ago. On any family tree the chances are that two or three people will already have something about them online.

If they have an unusual name the name might be just be enough. Otherwise you will need to add what is called a modifier, that is another term to narrow down the search, such as a place "London" or time "1854". You will also need to put your ancestors' fore and surnames into double quotes, such as "Paul Belcher". You may also need to exercise some patience and scroll through several pages before you find the ancestor you want.

Google, however, is more, much more, than just a search engine. It is, for example, busy scanning old books and there are millions of illustrations. On Google's home page www.google.co.uk click on 'more' and then follow the links to books. On the books page, type in the name and see what comes up. For copyright reasons not all books are available in full view, sometimes there is a just a snippet or even no views at all.

Google is not the only search engine available, although it is by far the largest. Microsoft's Bing (www.bing.com) is also worth checking out as often it come up with different results. Or you can search across all search engines at www.dogpile.com.

Other sites available include:

- My Heritage – www.myheritage.com (includes a great piece of software which allows you to see whether you or your ancestors look like a celebrity – apparently I look like Charles de Gaulle!)
- Lost Cousins – www.lostcousins.com (connects cousins through the ninteeenth-century censuses)

Chapter 3

USING ARCHIVES AND LIBRARIES

Eventually you will have to use original archive material, which may prove initially to be scary but once you overcome your nerves they can be deeply addictive and very rewarding.

These records are generally kept in specialist archives or record offices, rather than in libraries or museums (although there are often links between the three). Each record office has a different system of managing its records, although they all follow the same principles of archive administration that is documents are kept together by collection, rather than rearranged by subject as happens in a library.

There are hundreds of archives across the British Isles ranging in size from purpose-built repositories storing millions of documents to small rooms with just a few thousand items.

Card catalogues can be a useful finding aid in archives. Author's collection

It can sometimes be hard to find which records are held where, but a rough rule of thumb is that records created by central government are at National Archives in London (for the United Kingdom as a whole as well as England and Wales), Edinburgh (Scotland), Belfast (Northern Ireland) and Dublin (Ireland pre-1922 and the South), those by local government at county or city record offices, and records of many organisations also at county record offices. There are also a large number of specialist repositories for businesses, universities and charities that may (just possibly) have information.

Finding what survives and where the records are stored can be a nightmare. Fortunately help is at hand in the form of three databases provided by The National Archives. The National Register of Archives (www.nationalarchives.gov.uk/nra) lists most collections stored at local record offices, some museums and specialist repositories. An easier to use alternative is the Access to Archives (A2A) database (www.nationalarchives.gov.uk/a2a). Unfortunately, A2A is by no means complete and apparently is not being updated. Meanwhile ARCHON (www.nationalarchives.gov.uk/archon) provides links to local archive websites and provides addresses and other details about a bewildering range of archives great and small.

The National Archives

If you have been doing any research online the chances are that you were using records from The National Archives without knowing it. The vast majority of the archival material you will consult in your researches can be found at the Archives' headquarters at Kew in south-west London. Increasingly you don't need to come to Kew (although I hope that you will do so at some stage) because as you have probably discovered many of the most important records are now available online.

The National Archives (TNA) houses the surviving records of central government of the United Kingdom. Founded in 1838 as the Public Record Office (PRO), it now holds something like ten million documents, from the Domesday Book to records created by the Chilcot Inquiry on Iraq which took place in 2009 and 2010.

Among the records you may need to use are:

• Army service records (1760–1919)
• Census records (1841–1911)
• Criminal records (including records of trials and punishments)

The entrance to the National Archives at Kew. The Author

- Inward and outward bound passenger lists (1878–1960)
- Merchant seamen service and shipping records (1747–1970s)
- Metropolitan Police service records (1828–c1939)
- Naval service records (1852–c1920)
- Non-conformist birth, marriage and death registers (16th century-c1837)
- Operational records for the armed services (particularly for the world wars)
- Railway workers (1830–1948)

- Wills (15th century–1858)
  These records are described in more detail elsewhere in this book.

Three major series of records TNA does not hold are:

- Birth, marriage and death records from 1837 which are with the General Register Office
- Wills after 1858, which are with HM Courts Service
- Records relating to the British involvement in India from 1600 to 1947, which are at the British Library

And although there are many useful poor law and criminals records at Kew if you are tracing an ancestor who was a criminal or pauper a local record office is probably a better place to start.

It certainly helps to know how the 10 million or so records are arranged, particularly if you plan to visit Kew. Fortunately this is simple. The records

A box at The National Archives containing war diaries. Who knows what treasures will be found here!
The Author

are initially arranged by department (sometimes called lettercode), such as the War Office (which has the prefix WO) or Admiralty (ADM). The types of records are arranged by series (or classes) which is assigned a number, so war diaries for the First World War are in series WO 95, Militia Attestation Papers (1806–1915) are in WO 96, and Soldiers' Service Documents (1760–1913) are in WO 97. And individual units of production, known as pieces, are assigned a further unique number, so the war diary for 38 Trench Mortar Battery for July to October 1915 is in piece WO 95/1598, which happens to be a loose-bound file of papers one of a number kept in a large brown box, but other pieces might well be books, volumes of bound papers or even parchment rolls.

TNA's website is one of the key family history resources online. The address is www.nationalarchives.gov.uk. At time of writing everything is organised in five tabs – About Us; Education; Records; Information Management; and Shop Online – although this may change as the website evolves over time. "About

VISITING THE NATIONAL ARCHIVES

You are very welcome to visit The National Archives. As well as the records and the various reading rooms, there is a restaurant, an excellent book shop and interesting small museum. TNA is about ten minutes walk from Kew Gardens station and situated just off the South Circular Road (A205) in Bessant Drive. There is a car park (with a £5 per day charge).

Using the Archives, however, is free. You only need a reader's ticket if you are planning to use original records rather than material that is available online or on microfilm, A reader's ticket is valid for three years and entitles you to see anything which is publicly available. If you think you will need a ticket don't forget to bring two forms of identity – one to confirm your identity (such as a driving licence or passport) and one to confirm an address (such as a utility bill). Details at www.national archives.gov.uk/visit/when-you-arrive.htm

Visiting can be a daunting experience, but remember that the staff are both knowledgeable and friendly, and everything is arranged as simply as possible. Even so it is a good idea to allow plenty of time to find your feet.

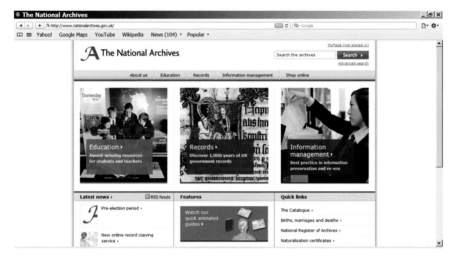

The homepage of The National Archives website. TNA

Us" provides information about The National Archives as a whole and has pages about visiting Kew as a researcher.

Of more immediate use is the "Records" tab which has links to various databases – including the main catalogue – and reference guides which will help you find what you want as well as understand what you are looking for and what the records will tell you. There are also links to the National Register of Archives, ARCHON and A2A databases mentioned above, as well as to Documents Online (see Chapter 2).

Of particular interest are the Research Signposts – some 150 excellent short guides to tracing people, places and subjects – which simply describe how to conduct particular searches with links to the catalogue and other websites as appropriate. Also worth checking out are the excellent short videos on a variety of topics from how to conduct research to how to order a document (look under "Quick Animated Guides").

More detailed information about the records can be found in the in depth Research Guides. Again the Records tab will take you to them. Some are better than others, while many are very technical, but they can still be very useful.

At the heart of The National Archives website is the Catalogue which describes each of the ten million or so documents at Kew. What's more it

The Research Signposts are useful introductions to many of the records held by The National Archives. TNA

Short videos can show you how to effectively use The National Archives. TNA

WHEN NOT TO SEARCH

On the homepage of The National Archives website there is a search engine. You may want to enter a name or phrase into it. However, this should be resisted, because if you do it will search all of the resources on the website and present you with hundreds, possibly thousands of indigestible results. So unless you are prepared to search for something very specific or are happy to wade through page after page of irrelevant entries, know what you are doing or are very lucky you should avoid the temptation.

incorporates an increasing number of databases for particular collections providing details of individuals, such as the gallantry awards made to individual merchant seamen during the Second World War. However, it is important to remember that details for only a fraction of individuals who appear in the records are yet available through the catalogue. You certainly can search for your ancestor here, but you MUST NOT assume because there is no entry for an individual there is nothing at The National Archives about them. It is also worth checking the catalogue every few months or so because more entries are being added all the time.

The catalogue is easy to use – just enter the search term into the "word or phrase" box. You can modify your search by year or by department. For example if you are looking for a particular war diary it is likely to be under the WO – or War Office – lettercode. If you want to know more there is a short video under the Quick Animated Guide tab.

Other archives

Each English and most Welsh counties has a county record office or archive service. In addition a few cities, like Portsmouth and Southampton, also maintain an archive. What they hold varies somewhat, but they are likely to have:

- Collections of papers from local companies, charities and organisations
- Local courts (particularly Quarter and Petty Sessions)
- Local government records
- Parish registers
- Poor law and workhouse records

Hull History Centre opened at the beginning of 2010. University of Hull

The best way to find out about their collections is generally from their websites. Some websites are superb and extremely informative, while others are very basic, but in general they should tell you about their holdings and provide leaflets which you can download about particular records or collections. A few have their own online catalogue (which are often hard to use). The website will also provide details of opening hours, which is important to note as most only open three or four days a week, location and the identification you need to bring to get a reader's ticket. Some archives are members of the CARN scheme where one ticket is valid in the reading rooms of all members.

Also of interest may be local studies libraries (sometimes called local history libraries or history centres) which are neither quite an archive nor really a library but contain elements of both. They are likely to have a comprehensive collection of books about the locality, including street directories. For researchers their greatest asset is often a comprehensively indexed collection of press cuttings from local, and sometimes national, newspapers going back to before the First World War.

The reading room at Wolverhampton Archives and Local Studies Library. Wolverhampton City Council

Local studies libraries are normally part of the central reference library, but many are being merged with the local record office as has been the case in Gloucestershire and Norfolk. The new Hull History Centre combines collections from the local city archive, the local studies library and uniquely Hull University's archives.

There are also a large number of smaller more specialist archives who may have material about your ancestors. Most large companies for example have an archive where staff registers and ephemera are stored. One of the best is Marks & Spencer's where a purpose-built archive is due to open at Leeds University in 2011. And if you are researching soldier ancestors (particularly officers) then you should find regimental archives useful.

Libraries

The largest library of them all is the British Library (BL) which until recently was wary of non-academic readers. They will normally only give you a reader's ticket if you can prove that the material you want to see is to be

The main entrance to the British Library building in London. British Library

found nowhere else. The British Library has the largest collection of books and manuscripts in the country. One copy of every book and journal has by law to be deposited with them. The manuscript collection is equally impressive with a vast hotchpotch of material from medieval land deeds to the papers of modern politicians. Family historians might want to use the Library in particular to look at:

- Newspapers – the British Newspaper Library which has copies of most newspapers, magazines and journals published in Britain since the seventeenth century. (See chapter 10)
- Indian material – if your ancestors worked for the Raj in India then this is the place to come (see chapter 9)

You can find out more at www.bl.uk.

USE YOUR LOCAL LIBRARY

Local libraries are an under-used resource for family historians. They may have many of the more detailed books you might need to consult in your research and should be able to get almost any out-of-print book for you through the Inter-Library Loan Service for a few pounds.

They also have an increasing number of online resources. If you haven't got the internet at home they have computers linked to the web. Many libraries also subscribe to Ancestry (and a very few have the 1911 census as well) which will be particularly useful if you want to do a few simple searches, but don't want to subscribe. Lastly, they may well be services available to subscribers online at home. Richmond-upon-Thames, where I live, for example, provides access to the *Oxford Dictionary of National Biography*, *Who's Who* and *The Times Digital Archive*, all of which have proved to be very useful over the years. Your council's website should indicate what is available.

The Society of Genealogists maintains a specialist library for family history at their premises in Clerkenwell. As well as the usual genealogical resources there is a superb collection relating to parish registers, publications of local record societies and school registers and histories. Unless you are a member there is an admission charge. A catalogue to holdings can be found on the Society's website www.sog.org.uk.

UNDERTAKING RESEARCH

Visiting an archive for the first time can be a daunting experience, partly because they are all arranged differently but mainly because everybody also appears to know what they are doing. However, almost without exception, record offices are extremely welcoming and are used to having novice visitors.

It is a good idea to ring before hand to book a seat – as most archives have very cramped reading areas. They should also be able to give you a rough idea whether they have the records you are interested in, indeed may have something ready when you arrive. The archivist can also tell you whether they allow the use of laptop computers, digital cameras and other gadgets.

You should take with you a notebook, several pencils (as pens are not allowed into reading rooms), any notes you might have, change for a locker

FAMILY HISTORY CENTRES

For doctrinal reasons the Church of Jesus Christ of Latter-day Saints (better known as the Mormons or LDS Church) encourages its members to research their ancestors. To help them do this they have invested huge sums in copying genealogical records from around the world which are available to patrons at the Family History Centre in Salt Lake City. Beyond a doubt the Library is the biggest genealogical research centre in the world. The resources of the Library are available to anybody (not just co-religionists) through a worldwide network of local family history centres. There are forty or so family history centres scattered across the British Isles, the largest of which is opposite the Science Museum in South Kensington. You can find their details at www.familysearch.org: the website also contains the Library's catalogue so you can see exactly what is available. As they are run by volunteers opening hours can be restricted so you need to check before you visit. The volunteers can help you with your research (although they do not claim to be experts) and you can order any film from the main library in Salt Lake City for a nominal amount. Find out more at: www.londonfhc.org

In addition, a number of local family history societies run research centres where members can use the society's resources (and non-members may be welcome on the payment of a small fee). They can be very useful if all your ancestors come from a particular area. Details are normally found on society websites.

The world's biggest Family History Library in Salt Lake City. Genealogical Society of Utah

Undertaking research at The National Archives. The Author

for your bag and coat (should they be provided). It is a good idea to allow plenty of time to familiarise yourself with the archive and its finding aids, particularly if you are going to make several visits. You may also want to talk through what you hope to find with the archivist or librarian on duty, as they may be able to suggest places to look and shortcuts to take.

Most record offices allow you to take a digital camera to take shots of pages from documents, photographs and maps for your personal use. This can save both time in making notes, and cost in ordering photocopies. As each archive has its own rules, you should ask before snapping.

Written sources are the basis of all historical research. Using them properly makes the best use of your time and ensures that you get all you can from the records. You should:

- Note down all the references of the documents you consult, together with their descriptions, even for those items which were useless. You may need to use them again; having the references can cut the work in half
- Read each document thoroughly, especially if you are unfamiliar with the type of record. See whether there is an index at the front or back which might help you find your man
- Many records come in similar forms. Wills or war diaries, for example, all use much the same format. Once you have mastered the style they are easy to go through.
- There may be an index or other finding aid. This may not always be obvious, so ask the staff
- If you are not sure about how to use a document, ask the staff. They are there to help!

Chapter 4

RECORDS OF BIRTHS, MARRIAGES AND DEATHS

REGISTRATION CERTIFICATES

B irth, marriage and death certificates are the most important records you will use in the course of your researches. In England and Wales they start on 1 July 1837. Certificates were introduced because it was increasingly important that there be a legally recognised national system of registration. From the sixteenth century, Anglican churches had kept records of baptisms, marriages and funerals (see below), but not everybody worshipped in church. And the old system was clearly breaking down in the rapidly growing industrial towns where there were few churches or chapels.

The system introduced in 1837 remains much the same today: as you will know if you have ever been married or registered a birth or death. These events are registered at a local register office (or where appropriate a church for marriages). From here, superintendent registrars send copies of entries in the registers to the General Register Office (GRO) every quarter, that is at the end of March, June, September and December. At the GRO a comprehensive national index is compiled for each birth, marriage and death registered in the previous quarter, so births, marriages and deaths which took place in January, February and March appear in the March quarter. This is widely available online and on microfilm.

Ordering a certificate is simple although not quite as straightforward as you might imagine. It is not possible to see the certificate without paying for it, so buying them can be a bit of a lottery. The more you know before you order the better. In particular you need to have details of:

- Date when the event took place. This doesn't have to be exact, but the more information you have about the event the easier it becomes
- Place where the event took place. In general this is clear but remember that most large towns had two or more registration districts, for example in Liverpool West Derby covered most of the eastern suburbs.
- Name of the individual (of course)

BIRTHS REGISTERED IN OCTOBER, NOVEMBER, DECEMBER, 1861

NAME		SUP-REGISTRARS DISTRICT	VOL	PAGE
CROWL	Elizabeth	Tavistock	5b	3?6
	Male	St Austell	5c	4?8
CROWLE?	Odessa	Truro	5c	15?
	Philippa	St Columb	5c	1?7
	William Henry	Redruth	5c	2?5
CROWLEY	Agnes Eliza	Brentford	3a	1?7
	Daniel	Whitechapel	4c	3?1
	Elizabeth	Atherstone	6d	3?5
	Elizabeth	Atherstone	6d	3?1
	Elizabeth	Burnley	8e	4?8
	Emma	Aston	6d	2?7
	Jane	Birmingham	6d	(4?
	John	Ashton	8d	4?7
	John Denis	Kensington	1a	4?7
	Margaret	Brighton	2b	1?9
	Margaret	St Geo East	1c	4??
	Mary	Pontypool	11a	4?5
	Mary Ann	E London	1c	5?0
	Matthew Charles	Bristol	6a	?5
	Michael	Kensington	1a	7?8
	Robert	S Shields	10a	4?4
	Samuel	Kings N	6?	4?4
	Thomas William	Aston	6d	2?3
CROWLE?	Daniel	Merthyr T	11a	3?3
CROWNSHAW	Rose	Wortley	9?	1?2
CROWSHAW	Arthur	Atherstone	6d	3?1
	James	Bury	8?	4?3
CROWSON	Charlotte Ann	Caistor	7?	5?9
	Edith	Rotherhithe	11	5?9
	Edwin	Marylebone	1a	4?4
	Elizabeth	Malling	2?	3?6
	Emma	Oundle	3?	1?9
	Lydia Augusta	Islington	1?	2?5
	Mary Ritch	S Shields	10a	4?3
	Walter Harper	St Geo East	1?	4?7
	William	Pancras	1?	?9
CROWTHER	Abigail	Huddersfield	9?	3?7
	Albert	Halifax	9?	?6?
	Alfred	Wakefield	9?	?6
	Alfred	Huddersfield	9?	3?1
	Ann	Huddersfield	9?	5?6
	Ann Tyson	Whitehaven	10?	4?3
	Annie	Oldham	8?	5?3
	Aquilla	Halifax	9?	4?5
	Catherine	Auckland	10?	1?7
	Edward Samuel Dashwood	Droitwich	6?	3?5
	Eli	Halifax	9?	4?3
	Eliza	Ashton	8?	3?2
	Esquire Osvald Egerton	Barnsley	9?	11?
	Frederick George	Lewisham	1d	7??
	George	Manchester	8d	2??
	George Roberts	Halifax	9a	3??
	Henrietta Alicia	Bakewell	7?	5??
	Horsefield	Halifax	9?	4??
	James	Manchester	8d	2??
	John	Pontypool	11?	1??
	John Frederick	Manchester	8d	3??
	John Henry	Halifax	9?	4??
	John Stephen	Chelsea	1?	16?
	John William	Wigan	8?	8?
	Jonathan	Blackburn	8?	28?
	Joseph	Bradford Yk	9?	?6
	Joseph	Halifax	9?	363
	Joseph	Hunslet	9?	218
	Judith	Halifax	9?	365
	Laura Annie	Chorlton	8?	552
	Levina	Birkenhead	8?	561
	Luciana	Bradford Yk	9?	28
	Lydia	Halifax	9?	356
	Mary Elizabeth	Salford	8?	?9
	Mary Emma	Dewsbury	9?	4?5
	Mary Jane	Todmorden	9?	?95
	Matilda	Ludlow	6?	505
	Morton	Huddersfield	9?	506
	Oliver	Huddersfield	9?	3?1
	Sar	Huddersfield	9?	3?4
	Samuel	Dailey	6c	36
	Sarah	Halifax	9a	355
	Sarah Ann	Bradford Yk	9b	4

NAME		SUP-REGISTRARS DISTRICT	VOL	PAGE
CROWTHER	Sarah Ann	W Derby	8b	383
	Sarah Jane	Huddersfield	9a	326
	Susannah	Haslingden	8e	108
	Thomas	Huddersfield	9a	330
	Thomas	Ashton	8d	352
	Thomas Crossley	Halifax	9a	440
	Thomas Edward	Blackburn	8e	274
	Thomas Edwin	Oldham	81	560
	Tom	Bradford Yk	9b	16
	Whiteley	Halifax	9a	421
	William	Manchester	81	209
	William	Penkridge	6b	341
	William	Bromsgrove	6c	35?
	William	Shoreditch	1c	85
	William Albert	Rochdale	8a	6?
CROWTON	Emma	Birmingham	6d	110
CROXALL	Henry Tomlinson	Bradford Yk	9b	10?
	James	Walsall	6b	493
	Olivia Malvina	Walsall	6b	52?
	Edwin	Thame	3a	491
	Sarah Jane	Driffield	9d	245
	Sarah Mary Ann	Leighton B	3b	35?
CROXEN	Edward Alfred	St Austell	5c	143
CROXTON	Ada	? Derby	8b	?96
CROYDON	Mary Ann	Honiton	5b	17
	Rosanna	Dudley	6c	78
	Nelson	Oldham	8d	529
CROYSDALE	Jane Ann	Bridlington	9d	269
CROZER	Frederic Edward	Westminster	1d	285
CROZIER	Alfred	Braintree	4a	311
	Alice	Gateshead	10?	162
	Ann Louise	Pancras	1b	162
	Anne	Lincoln	7a	427
	Elizabeth	Poplar	1c	615
	Josiah	Braintree	4a	309
	Margaret Ann	Castle W	10b	192
	Mary Ann	Castle W	10b	195
	Mary Ann	Durham	10a	226
	Mary Jane	Wigton	10b	411
	William Daniel	Longtown	10b	367
CRUCEFIX	Henry John	St Martin	1a	326
CRUCHLEY	Female	Chelsea	1a	17?
CRUCIFIX	Garton Joseph	Manchester	8c	28?
CRUIREIX	John	Mile End	1c	51?
CRUICE	Ann	Liverpool	8b	153
	Mary Elizabeth	Liverpool	8b	45
CRUICKSHANK	Frederick	Westminster	1h	315
	Henry Robert	W Derby	8b	393
	Jane	S Shields	10a	502
	William	Westminster	1a	315
	Eliza	Gt Boughton	8a	31?
CRUISA	Francis	Tynemouth	10b	109
CRUM	Alfred Ebenezer	Monrouth	11a	43
	Edwin	Newport M	11a	16?
CRUMB	William	Chepstow	11a	3
CRUMBIE	Daniel	Tynemouth	10b	11?
CRUMMACK	Dick	Leeds	9b	301
CRUMPY	Ann	Gateshead	10a	533
CRUMP	Alfred William	Bermondsey	1d	7?
	Benjamin George	Leominster	6a	495
	Charles Ernest	Dudley	6c	46
	Edward	Wellington Sh	6a	712
	Elizabeth	St Saviour	1d	10
	Emily	Thanet	2a	629
	Emma	Stourbridge	6c	152
	Esther	Dudley	6c	20
	Esther Ellen	Bromsgrove	6c	354
	Frederick9	Dudley	6c	63
	George Henry	Monmouth	11a	34
	George Thomas	Islington	1b	218
	Harrdyman Fieldhouse	Wellington Sh	6a	712
	Harry	Birmingham	6d	209
	Henry	Barnsley	9c	133
	Jabez Arthur	Chesterfield	7b	502
	James	Dudley	6c	131
	John	Marylebone	1a	440
	John	Atcham	6a	60?
	Mary	Kidderminster	6c	213
	Mary Elizabeth	Pershore	5c	209
	Richard Henry	W Bromwich	6b	60?
	Sarah	Walsall	6b	493

A page from the GRO Indexes showing the birth of my great-grandmother Elizabeth Crozier in 1861. GRO/FreeBMD

Sets of GRO indexes are available on microfilm at Greater Manchester County Record Office, Birmingham Central Library, Bridgend Reference and Information Library, Plymouth Central Library and the City of Westminster Archives Centre. The Society of Genealogists also have an almost complete set. But The National Archives does not have a set.

However, it is much easier to search the indexes online. The best place to start is www.freebmd.org.uk which, as the name suggests, is free but more importantly has by far the best index. There are also several commercial sites offering GRO indexes, including www.genesreunited.com, www.ancestry.co.uk and www.findmypast.co.uk.

Once you have found the entry you should note down the reference number, that is

- registration district
- volume
- page number

This will help when ordering a certificate. However, the GRO no longer actually requires them if you are ordering by phone or online, but it certainly means that you are more likely to get the right one if you follow this process. And you will receive your certificate significantly quicker if you can supply these details.

You can order a copy of the certificate either online, telephone or by post. Each certificate costs £9.25. Order at www.gro.gov.uk/gro/content/certificates; ring 0845 603 7788, or write to GRO PO Box 2, Southport PR8 2JD.

What you will find

The details contained on a BIRTH certificate include:

- Name, date and place of birth. If a time is given then the birth was a multiple one. If the name is omitted then one had not been agreed by the parents
- Father's name (if given at time of registration), place of birth and occupation. If no father is given then the birth was illegitimate
- Mother's name, place of birth, maiden surname and, after 1984, occupation

(Registrations made before 1969 do not include details of the parents' place of birth and mother's occupation.)

CLUES IN CERTIFICATES

Certificates are not just vital because they give exact details of when ancestors were born, married and died, they also provide important clues to follow up. A birth certificate, for instance, names the father and mother (including her maiden name), their address and the father's occupation. Armed with this information, you can look for the parents' marriage certificate. A death certificate not only gives you an address, but could also lead to an obituary, a report in a local newspaper or possibly even a coroner's inquest.

Details contained on a MARRIAGE certificate include:

- Date and place of marriage
- Name, age and marital status of each of the spouses
- Occupation and usual address
- Name and occupation of each parties' father
- Names of the witnesses
- Name of the person who solemnised the marriage

If both bride and bridegroom were over the age of 21 this would be noted as "of full age". It is not unusual for ages to be changed either to make an individual appear older (particularly if they were under 21) or younger (perhaps to minimise a large disparity in ages between the spouses).

If the same address is given this is not generally because they were cohabiting. Either they gave the bride's address (occasionally the bridegroom's) so they could marry at her church, or they were "living" at an address for 21 days before the wedding so they could marry in the church of their choice, which might not be anywhere near where either spouse lived.

The witnesses were normally family members or friends, which could give further clues to relationships. In addition, if a cross was made by one or both of the parties this suggests that they were illiterate or at best very unused to writing.

The details contained on a DEATH certificate include:

- Name, date and place of death
- Date and place of birth (before 1969 a certificate only shows the age of deceased) If the individual died in a workhouse or hospital there may be further records worth tracking down.

- Occupation and usual address
- Cause of death. Alternatively if the cause of death was unusual or suspicious then a coroner's inquest should have been held. These are often covered in local newspapers. If you come across the phrase "visitation of God" this indicates that the individual died of unexplained natural causes
- The person who gave information for the death registration. If the informant was present at the time of death then this would be recorded

---

CAN'T FIND YOUR PERSON?

In particular, finding birth certificates can be tricky. The chances are they were registered – which was compulsory from 1874 and almost universally observed before then. These hints may help:

- The indexes are at fault (the national set of GRO indexes is very inaccurate). The answer may be to use the indexes kept by local registration offices which are generally better
- The name by which you know an ancestor is not the one he or she was given at birth. A old friend of mine was always known as Tig Vernon, but she was actually registered as Mary. You may find the correct name later in your research
- If you don't already have a date for a marriage, start looking around the date of the first known child's birth, then continue to search the indexes backwards in time, remembering that they could have married 20 or so years before then. If that fails, look forward from the birth date

Of course, it is quite possible that a couple never married. Until the late 1930s divorce was very difficult for ordinary people and many couples decided to separate without going through legal proceedings. As a result individuals could not legally remarry. The alternative was bigamy, which seems to have been reasonably common as the chances of being found out was remote. Alternatively couples just lived together. However as there was a social stigma to cohabitation the pair generally kept very quite about it.

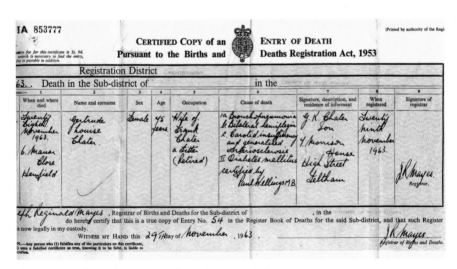

An example of a birth certificate. General Register Office

An example of a death certificate. General Register Office

An example of a marriage certificate. General Register Office

Alternatives

Inevitably you will need to buy a number of certificates in the course of your research, but there are other resources which may help reduce the cost or provide additional information:

- Local registration offices (see next page)
- Baptismal, marriage and burial registers are still kept by churches and chapels as they have been since before 1837 (see below). These registers are now largely deposited at local record offices. The information about marriage is identical to that on official certificates and baptismal entries are pretty informative. You will of course need to know at which church the event took place.
- Brief details of baptisms, marriages and deaths may given in parish magazines. These magazines began in the 1850s and by the end of the century most parishes and chapels produced them

- Local newspapers often include reports of marriages and funerals, with lists of those present and, where appropriate, photos of the happy couple. Also worth looking out for are the birth and death notices. (see Chapter 10)
- The National Probate Calendar provides details about testators (that is those who made wills) which duplicates information held on death certificates. At present it is available on microfilm between 1858 and 1943 in the Open Reading Room at The National Archives, the Society of Genealogists and other large libraries and archives. It is also available on Ancestry. (see Chapter 6)

LOCAL REGISTRATION

Provided you know where the event took place an alternative may be to approach the local registrar.

Generally they have copies of the events registered in their area back to 1837, although some registrars have passed older registers to the local record office. The staff are also likely to have more time to help. You can find addresses of local registration offices at www.direct.gov.uk (under "government, citizens and rights") or in the phone book. They are also listed in the *Family and Local History Handbook*, published annually by Robert Blatchford.

Increasingly, councils are putting their indexes online often with the help of local family history societies. But not the certificates, although there is usually a link to enable you to buy copies online. Many councils participate in the www.ukbmd.org.uk website, but by no means all. However, the site is the best place to start. There are many other family history resources available so it is worth visiting in any case.

There is another advantage to using local register offices. Buying certificates from them is slightly cheaper than from the General Register Office (£9 each rather than £9.25).

Originally based on poor law unions (the registrars were often the workhouse clerks) registration district boundaries have inevitably changed over the past 180 years. It can sometimes be hard to work out which villages or parishes were in which registration district. However, pages at www.ukbmd.org.uk/genuki/reg/ should be able to help.

MARRIAGE LICENCES

There are and were in fact two ways to get married in church. The first was by banns, whereby announcements are made in church of the forthcoming marriage for three successive Sundays before the happy day. Either the bride or the groom had to be resident in the parish. The alternative was by licence, that is by special permission of the church authorities.

Marriage by licence was regarded as the respectable way to marry. In part this was because it obviated the requirement that one at least of the parties had to live in a particular parish, which meant that it was possible to marry in the (fashionable) church of one's choice. Between 1618 and 1641 a quarter of all marriages at St Dunstan's Stepney, for example, were by licence.

It also allowed some degree of privacy because banns were not called. "Very few," reported a French visitor in 1697, "are willing to have their affairs declar'd to all the world in a publick place, when for a guinea they may do it snug."

In the eighteenth century probably one third of marriages were conducted by licence, although numbers fell off after the introduction of civil registration and changing social fashions. Now it is rare and the church frowns upon it.

The records of licences are allegations and bonds, which may provide more information than a parish register entry. A bond or deposit had to be entered into until 1823.

Licences were valid for three months. The associated oath (allegation) and bond provide a statement and undertaking of intention to marry and there are instances where the marriage did not actually take place. Sometimes the

DIVORCE RECORDS

Divorce was almost unheard off before 1857 when the first Divorce Act came into force and unusual and expensive until after the Second World War. Surviving records before 1938 are at The National Archives in series J 77. They have been indexed in the TNA Catalogue. Probably of more use (and certainly more entertaining) are newspaper accounts of court proceedings which often reveal the breakdown of the relationship in great detail.

It must be one of the most unusual marriages recorded in English parish registers: the wedding of Black Heart and Calls-the-Name, two Native Americans, at St Bride's in Stretford on 8 August 1891. The bride and groom were touring the North of England with Buffalo Bill's Wild West Show when they decided to marry. The register is now at Manchester Archives. Manchester Archives and Local Studies Centre

marriage took place at a different church from that mentioned in the allegation or bond. The records provide

- names of bride and groom
- the name or names of the church for which the licence is issued
- a note of consent by parent or guardian if either party is under age

However, it was not unknown for this to be falsified.

Licences could be granted by a variety of church authorities. If the bride and groom lived in different dioceses they had to apply to the Archbishop of Canterbury's Vicar General. If they lived in different provinces (York and Canterbury) they had to obtain a Faculty Office licence. The rules were often ignored, however.

Archbishops' licences are held at Lambeth Palace Library. They begin in 1534. Indexes between 1694 and 1850 are online at www.origins.net or through LDS family history centres and at the Society of Genealogists. The indexes contain nearly 400,000 names

Otherwise, records are likely to be found in diocesan records which are normally at local record offices, although ones for the Archdiocese of York are at the Borthwick Institute in York (www.york.ac.uk/inst/bihr). For example licences issued by the Bishop of London from 1521 are at the London Metropolitan Archives. Access online is patchy – the best collection is at www.origins.net, although those for London between 1597 and 1700 are on Ancestry. Otherwise there may be published indexes.

Further reading:
An excellent leaflet describing the records and their uses is at: www.york.ac.uk/inst/bihr/guideleaflets/marriagebondguidance.pdf

PARISH REGISTERS

Introduction

As you start to trace your ancestors back to the early nineteenth century and beyond you'll increasingly have to rely on parish registers. However, the records were often poorly kept or just do not survive which can make using them very frustrating, although there are several comprehensive name indexes.

The Anglican, or Church of England, was by law the established church. Until 1837 it was compulsory to baptise children, get married and be buried by the Church. It was also responsible for proving wills and had a role in running secular affairs in rural parishes.

There were (and indeed still are) some 16,000 parishes across England and Wales – most villages were within a single parish, although towns had two or more parishes generally depending on their size and the wealth of benefactors in medieval times. It was claimed in Norwich for example that it had a church for every Sunday of the year (as well as enough pubs for every day).

Each parish elected two churchwardens and in larger or wealthier districts appointed a clerk who was responsible for maintaining the registers. If the clergy and their clerks were conscientious then that is a great bonus for family historians. However, this was not always the case. In Richmond, Surrey the same family held the post of clerk for decades who, according to the transcriber of the records, "passed on the each generation to the next, a tradition of slovenliness and neglect in regard to their duty". This meant of course that many baptisms, marriages and deaths were either not recorded or incompletely noted in the register and are thus lost for good.

Although the Church of England was the only legal church, it does not mean that there are not other faiths. Roman Catholics, for example, did not entirely disappear with the Reformation in the sixteenth century. Despite terrible persecution parts of south Lancashire remained loyal to the old religion as did odd pockets elsewhere, especially where a local landowning family remained believers. A bigger threat to the Anglican Church however came from newer denominations. These nonconformists, as they were known, began with the Quakers and Baptists in the mid-seventeenth century. The most important faith however was the Methodists led by John Wesley, who came to prominence in the eighteenth century.

All this means that you may need to check the records of these other faiths as well as the Anglican parish registers to find your ancestors.

The Church of England

Parish registers were first kept in 1538 and of course are maintained today. Few records however survive before the beginning of the seventeenth century. The only major change since then was the introduction of printed forms in 1754 (for marriages) and 1813 for (baptisms and funerals) in which specified details have to be completed.

The survival of early registers is patchy, and they can be depressingly unhelpful. Baptismal entries are often little more than the child's name, who the father was, and when the event took place. Baptisms normally occurred within a few days of the birth. If the child was born out of wedlock this would also be noted and the mother's name given.

Before 1754, entries for weddings usually contain the names of the spouses, with perhaps a note if one of them was born outside the parish. After 1754, however, marriage entries had to be entered in special registers and are a little more informative. Death registers normally just contain the name of the deceased, although occasionally their age and occupation is noted.

Matters are made worse by the few Christian names which were in general use (most boys were called John, William, Henry, Thomas or George; girls: Mary, Elizabeth, Catherine or Anne). You may well find three or four babies with the same forename and surname christened within a few months of each other, making it impossible to work out from whom you are descended.

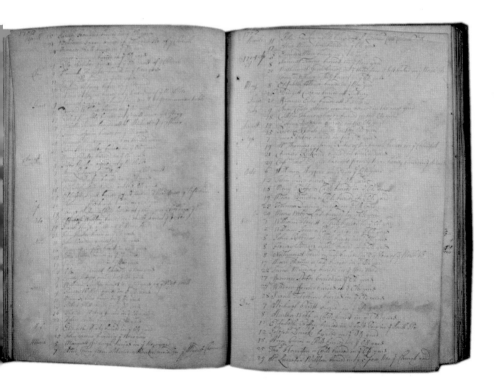

The baptismal entry for Thomas son of Joseph and Sarah Kensit in the printed baptism registers introduced in 1812. Ancestry/London Metropolitan Archives

The burial register for Clapham parish church in London with the entry for Samuel Pepys on 4 June 1703 (died 26 May). Ancestry/London Metropolitan Archives

A page from the transcript of the parish register for Richmond, Surrey. Surrey Parish Register Society

RICHMOND, SURREY.   73

1679-80	Jan.	2	William son of S^r Ja. Rushout, knt., and dame Alice his wife.
		5	Elizabeth dau. of Thomas Stanley.
		14	Henry son of Henry Hobbs.
		18	Roger son of Roger Gravenor.
		22	William son of John Gibson.
		30	John son of Nicholas Gaines.
		,,	John son of Walter White.
		31	Mary dau. of Humphry Jyncks.
	Feb.	8	William son of Richard Mounteney, esq^r, and Mary his wife.
		,,	Mary dau. of Thomas Coleman.
		,,	Elizabeth dau. of Edward Greenburgh.
		9	William son of William Cox.
		29	Robert son of William Sherman.
	Mch.	4	Erasmus son of Ralph North.
		,,	Robert son of William Murden.
		5	[*blank*] dau. of Robert Raymond.
		9	Alice dau. of Charles Wickes.
		11	Benjamin son of Mr Benjamin Collyers.
		13	Richard son of Dr Richard Griffith.
		14	James son of John Webb.
		,,	[*blank*] of John Bauke.
		21	Israell dau. of James Hopkins.
1680	Apl.	2	Robert son of Mr Robert Brown.
		4	Thomas son of Clement Lord.
		18	James son of Richard Griffin.
		20	Charles son of Mr Charles Mossom.
		29	Frances dau. of Robert Palmer.
	May	25	James son of Gyles Steevens.
	June	1	Frances dau. of Mr John Howlett and Amy his wife.
		,,	Mary dau. of George Reeves.
		2	Mary dau. of Henry Eling.
		9	John son of John Darley.
	July	8	Joseph son of Mr Mathew Walker and Mary his wife.
		12	Lydea dau. of James Cogdell.
		18	Elizabeth dau. of Mr Dan^{ll} Brent, jun^r, and Jane his wife.
		,,	Penelope dau. of William Gravenor.
		24	Charles son of Mr Andrew Foster and Jane his wife.
	Aug.	1	Robert son of Mr John Fox and Mary his wife.
		8	Elizabeth dau. of Simon Darby.
		,,	Susanna dau. of John Plumbridge.
		15	Humphry son of Hump. Reare.
		18	Thomas son of Richard Toy.
		29	Daniel son of George Kitchin.

If the register you are looking for is missing, it is worth seeing whether a duplicate – or bishop's transcript – survives. Clerks had to make regular copies and send it to the bishop for safekeeping. However as they were not paid for this task, the quality of the transcript is often poor.

Most parish registers and bishop's transcripts are with local record offices. It is now very rare for individual churches to keep their old registers. *Phillimore's Atlas* will tell you where registers are held (and a lot more besides). Archives and local libraries will have copies.

A large number of registers have been transcribed and many have been published by local family or county record societies. The largest collection of these transcripts is with the Society of Genealogists.

There are several national indexes (although none are complete), of which the most important are:

- Boyd's Marriage Index includes details of about one marriage in eight between 1538 and 1837. Online at www.origins.net
- Family Search (often referred to as the International Genealogical Index (IGI)) covers christenings and to a lesser extent marriages. It is by no means complete (and it is find to hard which areas it is most thorough for) and not always accurate, but even so it is a very useful tool to help point you in the right direction. www.familysearch.org. It is supplemented by the British Isles Vital Records Index which contains many additional names, which unfortunately is not online although some material is at http://Pilot.familysearch.org, but can be consulted at local LDS Family History Centres, the Society of Genealogists and other libraries and archives.
- The National Burial Index seeks to complement Family Search by indexing burial registers. The third edition was published in 2010 on CD by the Federation of Family History Societies, although many entries are available online at www.findmypast.co.uk. Coverage is very patchy and is best for the period after 1813.

A comprehensive guide to getting the best from the indexes can be found at www.ancestor-search.info

The further back you go the more difficult it becomes, largely because there are far fewer documents and many, of course, have been lost over the centuries. If you can't find people in the parish registers – or the various national indexes to them – you might try the following sources:

- Many marriages before 1754 were not performed in parish churches in order to get around the need for banns and other petty regulations. The favourite place was the Liberty of the Fleet Prison in London, where these rules did not apply. It is thought that 230,000 marriages in total were celebrated in or about the prison. Legislation regarding marriages was tightened up by Hardwicke's Marriage Act of 1754, which said that marriages (except for Quakers and Jews) had to take place in an Anglican church after 21 days notice had been given. Registers from Fleet Prison and a few other centres are at The National Archives. Indexes are online at www.familysearch.org and digitised images at www.bmdregisters.co.uk If your ancestor was well to do, then these records may help.
- The date a will was proved can give a rough idea when and perhaps where a person died. Its contents can also offer useful clues. For more about wills see Chapter 6

- Property deeds and related records often include copies of marriage settlements and other documents which may give a clue about the marriage of individuals. These records are normally at local record offices.
- Details of middle and upper class births, marriages and deaths often appeared in the *Gentleman's Magazine*, which was first published in 1732. See Chapter 10

Nonconformists and Catholics

During the eighteenth century more and more people were attracted by other faiths, especially Methodism which seemed both to be more vital and answer doctrinal questions in a more contemporary way than the Church of England. In general they were tolerated although until 1829 only Anglicans could be officers in the forces or attend university. The position was very different for Roman Catholics who remained actively discriminated against until the end of the eighteenth century.

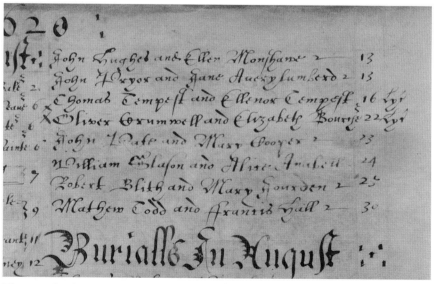

The entry for the marriage of Oliver Cromwell and Elizabeth Bourchier on 22 August 1620 in the parish register of St Giles Cripplegate, London (fourth line down). He was 21, she 22.
Ancestry/London Metropolitan Archives

Many nonconformists continued to use the parish church for christenings, marriages and funerals in order to stay within the law. In addition people often changed faiths at various times in their lives. A self-made businessman might start as a Methodist, but become a pillar of the Church of England once he made his fortune.

MONUMENTAL INSCRIPTIONS

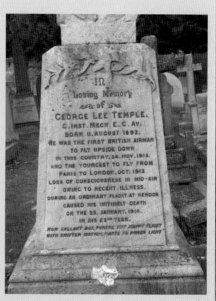

A gravestone from Acton Cemetery in London. The Author

Tombstones and monuments inside churches can provide useful information about the deceased and their family. Fortunately you don't have to go to where your ancestors are buried to get this information: although many people often find visits very moving. Most family history societies and a number of other bodies have visited local graveyards and noted down details of inscriptions on graves and monuments. A national collection of these monumental inscriptions, as they are called, is held by the Society of Genealogists. Local studies libraries and archives should have copies for their areas. An increasing proportion are available online through several websites including NAOMI (the National Archives of Monumental Inscriptions) at www.memorialinscriptions.org.uk (particularly for Bedfordshire and Norfolk) and the Gravestone Photographic Resource at www.gravestone photos.com (mainly Yorkshire).

For ancestors who are buried in municipal cemeteries, as increasing numbers were from the mid-nineteenth century, Deceased Online (www.deceasedonline.com) is worth checking out although not much is available at present.

On the setting up of the new central system of births, marriages and deaths in 1837, the government asked nonconformist churches to send in their registers, and most were happy to comply. These registers are now with The National Archives with indexes online at www.familysearch.org and the digitised registers themselves at www.bmdregisters.co.uk. A central registry, at Dr William's Library in London, also kept details of vital events submitted by individuals. Again these records are at The National Archives and www.bmdregisters.co.uk.

Registers for the period after 1837 have either been deposited with local record offices or are kept by individual churches or chapels. Some transcripts have been made and copies are often to be found at the Society of Genealogists (SoG).

Catholic churches were also asked to send in their registers, but relatively few did so. Indeed Catholicism was technically illegal until 1829; relatively few records survive. Most parish registers are still kept by the church. There are records of fines, and other penalties, imposed upon Recusants (that is those people who remained Catholics) at The National Archives and in Quarter Session records at local record offices. The SoG has transcripts of some parish records and other material about Catholics. The Catholic National Library also has considerable resources. For address see Appendix 3.

Further reading:

Michael Gandy, *Family History Culture and Faiths* (The National Archives, 2007)

Jeremy Gibson, *Bishops' Transcripts and Marriage Licences, Bonds and Allegations* (Federation of Family History Societies, 2001)

Cecil Humphrey-Smith, *The Phillimore Atlas and Index to Parish Registers* (Phillimore, 2002)

Patrick Palgrave Moore, *Understanding the History and Records of Non-Conformity* (Elvery Dowers Publications, 1994)

Stuart Raymond, *Parish Registers: a history and a guide* (Family History Partnership, 2010)

W E Tate, *The Parish Chest* (3rd edn, Cambridge University Press, 2008)

Chapter 5

THE CENSUS

Census records are some of the most important – and most interesting – records that you will come across in tracing your ancestors. They offer a fascinating snapshot of your family and the way they lived on a specific night. Indeed they will provide information you can't find elsewhere as well as clues which can lead to further research.

For each family member at home (plus servants and visitors) the census indicates their:

- Age
- Place of birth
- Occupation
- Relationship to the head of household (normally the oldest man)

As well as your direct ancestors you are likely to find information about:

- Other family members – particularly brothers and sisters of direct ancestors – you might not have come across before
- Servants and others staying in the household on census night

The first British census was held in 1801. With the exception of 1941, a census has been taken every ten years since. The first census act was passed by Parliament in November 1800 and it was taken just three months later – an incredibly short period of time. Local officials, found that nine million people lived in England and Wales although we do not who they were as few names or other individual details were collected. This was the pattern of the census until 1841.

By the late 1830s the Royal Statistical Society and others pressed for more detailed questions, although there was considerable opposition from people who feared an infringement of their civil liberties. The first census to contain details of every individual in Great Britain was taken in 1841. Because of these fears it is less informative than later ones. More detailed questions were asked in 1851 and at subsequent censuses.

CENSUS DATES

Census night was always a Saturday night and the householder was supposed to record everybody who was staying in his household on that night. The census was normally held in early spring when the movement of agricultural and other workers around the country looking for employment was thought to be at its lowest:

1801	10 March
1811	27 May
1821	28 May
1831	30 May
1841	6 June
1851	30 March
1861	7 April
1871	2 April
1881	3 April
1891	5 April
1901	31 March
1911	2 April
1921	19 June

Censuses are normally closed for 100 years. The only exception has been the 1911 census which was opened three years early in 2009 under the Freedom of Information Act. The 1921 census will be released in January 2022.

Up until 1911 officials, known as enumerators, distributed questionnaires a few days before census night to heads of household who were expected to complete them. They returned a few days later to collect the completed paperwork and to help people who were illiterate to fill in the forms. Once all the questionnaires had been collected the enumerator entered the details into books (known as Census Enumerators' Books or CEB) which were sent to Whitehall for processing. It is these books that form the basis of the census we are familiar with today. With very few exceptions the original forms have been destroyed.

The 1841 census for Derby. TNA HO 107/190 (Ancestry)

MAKE NO MISTAKE

You will often see marks on the forms which appear to be scorings out. These are the original pencil marks made by the civil servants as they went through the census books noting down the information for analysis and eventual publication as detailed books of statistics. Occasionally they obscure the information you are seeking – ages are particularly likely to be hidden in this way. The answer may be to look for copies of the census which have been filmed in colour rather than in black or white or greyscale where the marks are clearly shown in colour (generally red or blue).

THE MAN WHO REFUSES TO FILL UP THE SCHEDULE,
AND DEFIES THE ENUMERATOR.

A cartoon from the Illustrated London News *showing a problem faced by enumerators at the time of the 1891 census.* TNA ZPER 34/98

In 1911 a new system was introduced. The CEBs were no longer compiled. Instead the original forms completed and signed by the householder – generally the 'man of the family' – were collected and sent to London for processing by calculating machines.

The answers people provided are very informative about themselves and other members of their family. In addition they can lead you to other records, either to find out more about the people in the census or to take your search back in time.

From the census you can discover the following:

- Name
- Sex
- Marital state
- Age – in 1841 for adults over 14 years old, this was rounded down to the nearest five years although not all enumerators did this. If you were aged 47 on census night you would thus be entered as being 45.

A page from the 1851 census for the village of Benson near Oxford. TNA HO 107/1690 (Ancestry)

- Where people were on census night – even if they did not normally live there.
- Relationship to the head of the household – who was normally the oldest man
- Occupation – this can be misleading as often people had two or more jobs to make ends meet. Many pub landlords for example worked as small tradesmen to supplement their income. Children were commonly entered as 'scholars' although they may not actually have been at school
- Birthplace – in 1841 this was noted as being just in the county or outside it. From 1851 the parish and county of birth had to be included. For people born in Scotland, Ireland, or abroad it was sufficient just to put the country of birth, although often more details are included. It can sometimes be difficult to work out where people were born – either the details are incomplete or the parish given does not exist. This may be because the enumerator misheard what he was told

The entry for my grandmother Elizabeth Grace Crozier in the 1901 census. At the time she was living in Twickenham. TNA RG 13/673/Findmypast

SUPPLEMENTARY INCOME

For obvious reasons very few prostitutes indicate their professions in the census, although in Victorian and Edwardian England tens of thousands of young women engaged in 'the oldest trade'. Milliner was a common euphemism for a prostitute so if you come across an ancestor who made hats she may, just possibly, have supplemented her income on her back!

Most unusually the 1871 census for Albert Square in Tower Hamlets describes a number of local prostitutes. TNA RG 10/544 (Ancestry)

- Whether they were blind, deaf, dumb or insane. This information is at present obscured (or redacted to use the jargon) in the 1911 census under the terms of its early release. It will be made available in January 2012

In addition, in 1891 and 1901, people had to indicate

- Whether they were employed, self-employed, or unemployed. This question was often misunderstood, so the answers are unreliable

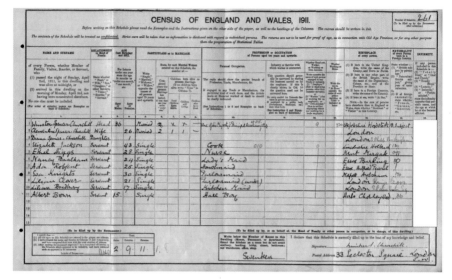

The entry for Winston Churchill in the 1911 census. These forms are radically different from anything which had previously been used for the census. The blanked out column contains details of any physical or mental disabilities. This information will be revealed in January 2012. TNA RG 14 (Findmypast)

- The number of rooms in each household if fewer than five
- In Wales whether they could speak Welsh, Welsh and English, or just English. Similar questions were asked in Scotland and Ireland

In 1911, householders also had to supply details of the:

- Length of time women had been married
- Number of children living and deceased
- The industry they worked in as well as the specific job
- Whether they had been naturalised
- The number of rooms in the house

In addition, the householder's signature appears on the form.

Getting access

All the censuses are now available online and most people use them in this way, because it is so much easier. Alternatively most local record offices and libraries have copies of the 1841–1891 (and often 1901) censuses on microfilm. The original census enumerators books are held by The National Archives but are not available to the public.

If you consulting the censuses online you may have the choice of looking at a digitalised image of the original page or a transcript, that is a copy, of the entry. The image is normally rather more expensive but is worth paying for because it is usually more informative and of course looks much better.

There are several commercial websites which have sets of censuses. In *Ancestors* magazine we conducted various tests over the years and came to the conclusion that they are all rather similar, the one you choose may depend on what other databases or services the data provider have or the deals they are offering. They are:

- www.ancestry.co.uk – 1841–1901 censuses. It is likely to add the 1911 census in 2011 or 2012. Some people have suggested the indexing is not particularly good, although personally I have found no problems;
- www.findmypast.co.uk – 1841–1911 censuses. At the time of writing the only one with the whole range of the censuses;
- www.genesreunited.com – 1841–1901 (likely to disappear they have recently been bought by Findmypast)
- www.thegenealogist.co.uk – 1841–1901 – claims to have the best indexes.

Using any of these websites is much the same. It is a matter of typing in the name of the ancestor you are looking for into the appropriate search engine together with various modifiers such as age, place of residence or spouse. Clearly the more information you have the easier it will be to find the person, but be warned if you type in <u>too much</u> you will confuse the search engine and it will not come up with a result. Even so, with common names you may need to go through several pages of entries to find the individual in whom you are interested.

CAN'T FIND YOUR ANCESTOR?

There may be several reasons why they do not appear to be in the census. The most important reason is that the surname may be spelt in a different way to that you were expecting, for two reasons:

- The name may have been written that way in the original
- The indexer may have misindexed the surname. Initially indexing was somewhat of a hit and miss affair, but things have improved markedly. If you do find an error please report it

There may be other reasons why you can't find your person:

- They may be at a different address on census night to the one that you expected;
- They gave the wrong details (ie wrong birth place) which may make it difficult for you to check that he or she is the right person;
- Their forenames may be different ie a John Willie Lees may be the Willie Lees or John Lees you are researching;
- Their age was different. As you trace people through the censuses you will see that their ages will often vary usually by two or three years between census. Men and women genuinely did not always know exactly when they were born – they had no need to because they rarely filled in forms, let alone received a pension;
- They were outside the country on census night. For censuses from 1891 it may be worth checking the outward bound and inward bound passenger lists (see Chapter 9) to see whether they can be found there;
- They may have been missed out by the enumerator. The authorities recognised that up to five per cent of people were not counted for one reason or another. Often they were sleeping rough or living on canal boats or in gypsy encampments. Most famously thousands of suffragettes refused to be enumerated in 1911 as a protest against women not having a vote
- Lastly the census might not survive or been copied – although this is very rare. Between five and ten percent of the 1861 census is thought to be missing and a small part of 1851 has also been lost

USING THE CENSUS FOR FREE

If you can't afford to subscribe to a commercial website, here are some alternatives:

- Ancestry is available for free at many local libraries;
- Most local archives and local studies libraries have the 1841–1891 censuses available on microfilm as well as the 1901 census on microfiche for their area. The 1911 census however will not be available in this way. Ask whether there are any street or name indexes which should make your search easier;
- The National Archives and the Society of Genealogists provide free access to all the censuses on site;
- Transcripts and indexes to the 1881 census are available at www.familysearch.org;
- Transcripts for an increasing number of places are at www.freecen. org.uk;
- Local history websites for particular villages or towns may have transcripts for certain census years

What the census can also tell you

As well as telling you about your direct ancestors, census records can provide other information, such as:

- Relations, lodgers and servants staying in the household
- If the relations of the wife are resident (and this is normally made clear in the relationship to the householder column) you may discover the wife's maiden name and perhaps something about her family as well.
- You can sometimes track the movement of the family around the country by the birthplace given for the children.
- Using the information in the birthplace column for the adults you can go to the parish registers for the individual to track down information about their christening (see Chapter 4).
- Information about the neighbours and an insight into the community in which your ancestors lived.

Abs.nt-minded Householder (who takes the Census returns very seriously). "AH, MARTHA JAMES—ER, WIDOW?—ER, AGE? H'M—THIRTY-FIVE, H'M—MALE OR FEMALE?"
Cook (indignantly). "FEMALE!"

A cartoon from Punch *for 26 March 1911. This must have been a not uncommon problem in many prosperous households!* Punch

Supplementary sources

Much of the information contained in the census returns is unique and cannot easily be found elsewhere. Even so the following may provide further information:

• Street or trade directories (see Chapter 10)

For the 1911 census there are two unique sources:

• Valuation office records (see Chapter 9)
• First World War service records (see Chapter 8)

NATIONAL IDENTITY CARD REGISTRATION

A census of the United Kingdom was due to be taken in early 1941 but this never happened because the government had greater concerns before them. However, a semi-census was conducted on the outbreak of war in order to provide an identity card for every man, woman and child in Great Britain, which helps to fill the gap. On Friday 29 September 1939 some 66,000 enumerators delivered forms to every household. On the Sunday and Monday following the enumerators returned, checked the form and there and then issued a completed identity card to each resident.

Looking at a National Identity Card. Paul Harris

Information gathered for each person was:

- Name
- Sex
- Date of birth
- Marital condition
- Occupation
- Whether he or she was a member of the armed forces or the reserves

Approximately 46 million cards were issued. It emerged subsequently that in some areas, a significant number of mothers had omitted their sons from the registration because they did not want them to be called up but later came forward to register them when they realised it was needed to obtain ration books.

The Identity Card was finally abolished in February 1952, but the identity numbers continued to be used within the National Health Service to give everyone an individual number. People who had a national identity number during the Second World War still have the same number as their NHS identity today.

The original records are now with the NHS Information Centre. A Freedom of Information ruling in 2009 gives partial access to the 1939 registration documents, but only for people who appear in it and are now dead.

If you want to have a search made of the records for England and Wales you need to contact the Centre. There is a charge for the provision of details of residents at a particular address of £42 (with no refund if the search is unsuccessful). For more information visit www.ic.nhs.uk/news-and-events/news/nhs-ic-launches-the-1939-register-service or write to The NHS Information Centre, The 1939 Register Team, Smedley Hydro Rm B108, Trafalgar Road, Birkdale, Southport PR8 2HH.

In Scotland you should contact Extract Services, General Register Office for Scotland, New Register House, 3 West Register Street Edinburgh EH1 3YT. Here the charge is a much more reasonable £13, but this is for a person search, not an address search. Again you need to prove that the person you are researching is deceased. Northern Ireland was initially excluded from the scheme.

For an excellent article about the Cards and the registration process visit www.1911census.org.uk/1939.htm

Further reading:

Dave Annal and Peter Christian, *The Census: The Expert Guide* (The National Archives, 2008)

John Hanson, *How to get the best from the 1911 census* (Society of Genealogists, 2010)

Stuart Raymond, *Census 1801–1911: A Guide for the Internet Era* (Family History Partnership, 2009)

Chapter 6

WILLS

Wills can provide a useful source for family history – describing the property and possessions held by the maker of the will, listing members of the family, friends and on occasion servants, and sometimes indicating what he or she thought of them. Academics are still puzzling over the meaning of Shakespeare's bequest of his 'second best bed' to his wife. Wills are of course important legal documents as they may be consulted generations after the death of the will-maker, to discern their instructions about the establishment or purpose of a trust or charity. This is why so many survive.

Until fairly recently wills however were only made by relatively small numbers of people: in 1900 only about one person in ten made a will. Most individuals had so little to leave that their possessions were divided up between their family without the need to trouble the law. Most wills were made when the individual (in legal terminology a testator or testatrix (woman)) was either very old or seriously ill.

The earliest wills date from the fourteenth century. The basic form has changed little since then, although modern wills are unlikely to include instructions for masses to be said in the will-makers name or commend the individual's soul to God's mercy. Before 1733 they were usually in Latin (as were most legal documents), but with a little practise it is fairly easy to pick out the key points.

Until 1882 all property belonging to a woman passed to her husband on marriage, so there are wills only for spinsters or widows.

The best and most comprehensive introduction to the subject is Karen Grannum and Nigel Taylor, *Using Wills* (The National Archives, 2007).

Wills before 1858

Finding wills before 1858 frankly is a minefield – and it may be the most complicated research you undertake, although the results can be very rewarding. There are at least four places where you might find a will, largely because probate was administered by a complex network of ecclesiastical courts as wills were supposed to be a contract between the testator and God. Where wills were proved basically depended on how rich the deceased was. Surviving records are at a number of local record offices.

In future help may be at hand in the form of a National Wills Index. A National Wills Index (www.nationalwillsindex.com) is being created by British Origins. The plan is to provide a unique single access point for all surviving pre-1858 wills, including the creation of new indexes and the digitisation of many surviving records.

The place to start, however, at present, is at The National Archives which has the records of the Prerogative Court of Canterbury (PCC). The PCC was the supreme ecclesiastical court covering the whole of England and Wales. If property was held in both north and south of the Trent, or just two or more dioceses south of the river, then property was proved here. The PCC also had jurisdiction over the estates of those who died abroad, including soldiers, sailors and West Indian planters. Perhaps more importantly, executors often had wills proved in courts higher than necessary, so during the first half of the nineteenth century there was a growing tendency to use the PCC for even relatively small wills, including those made by fairly humble people. Wills here date between 1384 and 12 January 1858.

The online index to the Prerogative Court of Canterbury wills. TNA

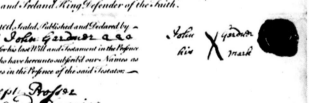

The will for the seaman James Gordon dated 1742 which proved in an probate court held by the Bishop of London. London Metropolitan Archives

The will for the Revd Paul Belcher which was proved in July 1823. TNA PROB 11/672

My Library of Books unto all and every my children Paul Thomas Michael Mary and Louisa the same to be equally divided amongst them at the sole discretion of my Executrices And as concerning all the rest residue and remainder of my monies goods personal estate and effects I give and bequeath the same unto my son Paul Belcher his executors and administrators Upon trust that he or they do and shall with all convenient speed convert the same into money and place such money out at interest upon Government or good and sufficient real security and pay and apply the interest dividends and produce thereof unto my son Thomas Belcher and his assigns during his life And from and immediately after the decease Upon trust to pay and divide the said trust monies and the funds and securities in or on which the same shall be invested unto all and every the third and children of my said son Thomas Belcher as and when they shall severally attain their respective ages of twenty one years with interest in the meantime for their maintenance and support And in case my said son Thomas Belcher shall die without leaving any lawful issue or being any such they shall all die before they shall attain their respective ages of twenty one years then upon trust that the said Paul Belcher his executors or administrators do and shall pay divide and transfer the said trust monies funds and securities equally between and amongst them share and share alike Provided always nevertheless

my said two daughters Mary and Louisa the same over and divided equally to be divided between and amongst

and I do hereby empower and direct my said son Paul Belcher his executors and administrators if he or they shall think it proper and expedient so to do and solely in his or their discretion to advance and pay any part not exceeding one half of the said trust monies unto my said son Thomas Belcher in his lifetime notwithstanding the limitations hereinbefore contained And it is my will and I do hereby direct that the said Legacy of One Thousand pounds given to my said son Michael Belcher shall bear lawful interest from the time of my decease until actual payment thereof And lastly I do hereby nominate and appoint my said two daughters Mary and Louisa joint Executrices of this my will hereby revoking all former wills by me made In witness whereof I the said Paul Belcher the testator have to the two first sheets of this my will set my hand and to this third and last sheet my hand and seal the day and year first above written P Belcher Signed sealed published and declared by the said Paul Belcher the testator as and for his last will and Testament in the presence of us who at the request in his presence and in the presence of each other have hereunto set our names as witnesses thereto R S Perkins Wm Dewes

Proved at London 16th July 1823 before the Judge by the oaths of Mary Belcher Spinster and Louisa Belcher Spinster the Daughters the Executrices to whom Admon was granted having been first sworn by Comon duly to Admy.

Ann Brewer

This is the last Will and Testament of me Ann Brewer late of Greyhound Row afterwards in Sight Row and now residing at No 4 Silver Street at the Gravel Pitts in the said Parish of Saint Mary Abbotts Kensington in the County of Middlesex widow who being at the time of making thereof of sound and disposing mind memory and understanding Do make publish and declare the same to be as follows that is to say I do hereby remise remit forgive release and discharge all and every my four children sons and daughters and the respective husbands of my daughters and their and all and every of their lands tenements goods chattels and estates of and from all such debt and debts as well simple contract or specialty which they or any of them respectively shall owe to or be indebted to me in or on respect of his or her or their executors or administrators and assigns and their and each or either and each and every of their have given security to me for at the time of my decease and to such as may have given any security to me for any debt or sum or sums of money

—by

The records themselves are available on online at www.nationalarchives. gov.uk/documentsonline and can be downloaded for a fee. There is an easy to use index, although of course it helps to know roughly when your ancestor died and the occupation he was engaged in.

The other main court was the Prerogative Court of York (PCY), which covered England north of the River Trent. Its records are at the Borthwick Institute of Historical Research, University of York, Heslington, York YO10 5DD, www.york.ac.uk/inst/bihr. However, many indexes are now available through British Origins at www.orgins.net, including those for the Prerogative and Exchequer Courts of York, 1731–1858, all the peculiar court indexes, and probate records before 1500.

There was also a network of bishops and archdeaconry courts which, in theory at least, proved wills of lesser amount. If you know where and when an ancestor died, it is not difficult to establish the court or courts which might have been used, and where the relevant records are kept. These records are usually at county record offices. *Probate Jurisdictions: Where to look for Wills* by Jeremy Gibson and Else Churchill (Federation of Family History Societies, 2002) is an indispensable guide to where the records are to be found. It is arranged on a county basis, and includes sketch maps; and it indicates the existence of any indexes, of which there are many, along with their location. In some cases there are calendars (that is summaries of the wills) or indexes. A few, particularly for London, are available at www.origins.net, while copies of most calendars and indexes are in the Society of Genealogists' library. Some local record offices have placed indexes online, such as the wills database for Cheshire at www.cheshire.gov.uk/Recordoffice/Wills and Gloucestershire www.gloucestershire.gov.uk/genealogy. Unfortunately many probate records for the West Country were destroyed during an air raid on Exeter in 1942. A project is underway to try to rebuild this collection – details at http://genuki. ce.ncl.ac.uk/DEV/DevonWillsProject.

Over 190,000 wills proven in Welsh ecclesiastical courts prior to 1858 have been digitised and made available by the National Library of Wales at http://tinyurl.com/yl3s9t9. Irritatingly the records cannot be downloaded; copies must be ordered from the library.

For about a century after 1670 the convention was to include an inventory with the will. These inventories list all the items belonging to the deceased room by room as well as outhouses such as farms, so you can get a very good idea of how a house was furnished and the resources the individual had to make his way in the world. Some are at The National Archives while others are at the Borthwick Institute and local record offices. There are few indexes, although an index for those at the Gloucestershire Record Office are online (see URL above).

THIS IS THE LAST WILL of me HUGH CRAWFORD of 21 Sudbrook Gardens Ham in the County of Surrey.

1. I REVOKE all wills and testamentary dispositions at any time heretofore made by me.

2. I APPOINT BARCLAYS BANK TRUST COMPANY LIMITED (hereinafter called "the Company") to be the EXECUTOR AND TRUSTEE of this my will and I DECLARE that the general terms and conditions upon which the Company acts as executor and trustee last published before the date hereof shall apply and be incorporated herein and the Company shall have the right to retain and be paid remuneration in accordance with the scale and other fees usually charged by it at the date of my death for its services in acting as executor and trustee of a will and shall have the option to retain and be paid remuneration in accordance with the scale and other fees usually charged by it from time to time (if and so far as altered after the date of my death) for such services as aforesaid.

I DESIRE that my solicitor Arthur David Macleod Robinson or his firm of Dixon Ward & Co. of 15/16 The Green Richmond Surrey shall be employed in the proof of my will and the administration of my estate and of the trusts hereof and that Arthur E. Kennett or his firm of Debenham & Chancellors also of Richmond aforesaid shall be employed in the sale of my house 21 Sudbrook Gardens aforesaid and any of my personal chattels which are not the subject of a specific gift hereunder.

3. I WISH to be cremated and my ashes scattered with the least possible expense unless there shall not be any convenient crematorium near to the place of my death in which event I wish to be buried where I die.

4. I GIVE the following pecuniary legacies all free of death duties:-

(a) The sum of five hundred pounds to the said Arthur David Macleod Robinson in appreciation of his friendship and help to me in business matters during my lifetime.

(b) The sum of five hundred pounds to Dr. Howard McLeish of 609 Upper Richmond Road West Richmond aforesaid in appreciation of many years of friendship.

(c) The sum of four thousand pounds to my godson Jonathan Peter Hugh Pine of Cedar Lodge Church Road Ham Common.

(d) The sum of ten thousand pounds to Mrs. Marguerite Anne Knight and the sum of three thousand pounds to Miss Ethel Harrison in recognition of their loyal and conscientious service in the running of my household and their care and attention to myself and to my late wife.

(e) The sum of two thousand pounds to my sister Nellie Malcolm.

(f) The sum of one thousand pounds to my half-brother Guy Crawford of Healsville near Melbourne South Australia.

(g) The sum of five hundred pounds to my wife's niece Norah Dorey c/o. P.O.Rosevears Tasmania.

(h) The sum of five hundred pounds to John (usually known as Jack) Burgess of Loch View South Scousburgh Shetland Isles.

(i) The sum of five hundred pounds to Robert Burgess (brother of the said Jack Burgess).

(j) The sum of five hundred pounds to Sinclair Moncrieff (son of John Moncrieff) of Spiggie South Scousburgh aforesaid.

(k) The sum of two hundred and fifty pounds each to George Robertson and Ian Robertson sons of Alec Robertson and both of the Nee Scousburgh aforesaid and I DECLARE that in the event of either of them the said George Robertson and Ian Robertson being a minor at the date of my death or when the said legacies shall be available for payment the Company may pay the said respective legacies to the parents or either of the parents of such minor whenafter the Company shall be discharged from all further responsibility therefor.

(l) The sum of two hundred pounds to William Burgess (known as "Hooly") of Souther House Scousburgh aforesaid.

5. I GIVE the following specific legacies free of all death duties:-

(a) To the said Jonathan Peter Hugh Pine my books and pictures (or any of them which he may wish to keep) my fishing tackle and my geological equipment and gear. The geological specimen cabinets and their contents already belong to him and accordingly do not form part of my estate.

An example of a modern will for Hugh Crawford of Richmond who died in 1971. Principal Probate Registry

Wills from 1858

A system similar to the registration of births, marriages and deaths was set up with a network of district probate registries feeding in wills to the Principle Probate Registry in London. Once a will has been proved it becomes a public record and with the exception of royal wills can be seen by anyone. However, despite various plans, no wills are yet online and are not likely to be in the immediate future.

The Principal Probate Registry can be found at First Avenue House, 44–49 High Holborn, London WC1V 6NP (Tel: 020–7947 6939), www.hmcourts-service.gov.uk. Opening hours are 10am to 4.30pm Mondays to Fridays. Wills cost £5 a copy and take up to a week to produce. Postal searches cost £5 for a

---

DEATH DUTIES

In 1796, a duty was imposed on the estates of deceased persons. Initially this only applied to a limited range of bequests outside the immediate family, but the scope of these death duties was gradually increased so that from 1815 almost all estates were included. As this was a national tax, the records are held centrally, as are the indexes. The Death Duty Register indexes are, therefore, the nearest equivalent to a national probate index before 1858. They are in annual volumes, and are only roughly arranged in alphabetical order. You can consult them on microfilm at The National Archives, in series IR 26 before 1858 (and IR 27 between 1858 and 1903). Indexes are online at www.findmypast.co.uk. Copies of registers between 1796 and 1811 only are at www.nationalarchives.gov.uk/documentsonline.

Each entry in the register gives the name and parishes, sometimes even the street addresses, of the testator and executor, the court where the will was proved, and a reference to the entry in the Death Duty Register itself. The registers can be difficult to interpret, as they contain many abbreviations, and as the original documents are double-page spreads in very large books, so they are not easy to read. However they are worth persevering with, as they can be very useful, providing details such as the full names and addresses of persons mentioned in the will, and even dates of marriage and death, where a bequest was conditional on marriage or coming of age, or an annuity which ceased on their death. Jane Cox's *Wills, Inventories and Death Duty Registers* (FFHS, 1993) is a good, if now dated, introduction to these records.

three year period, in addition to the fee for the will itself, and are carried out by the York Probate Sub-Registry. Write to The Postal Searches and Copies Department, The Probate Registry, 1st Floor, Castle Chambers, Clifford Street, York YO1 9RG; tel: 01904 666777. Applications for searches must be made in writing, and give the full name, last known address and date of death of the person concerned. A search can normally be made using less detail, but if the date of death is not known, you must state the year from which you want the search to be made, or give some other evidence that might indicate when the person died. At the time of writing, there is a considerable backlog so wills may take two or three months to arrive.

Unfortunately the Court Service does not seems to have discovered the potential of the internet to help customers so very little is online except some unhelpful leaflets.

Calendars (or registers), known as the National Probate Calendar, are provided for each year, which list all wills proved and give a reference number which you quote if you decide to order a will. These registers give the date of death, value of estate and who the executors (normally a member of the family) were. That is they give much the same information as a death certificate. And it's free! Copies of the calendars on microfiche, between 1858 and 1943, are available in the Open Reading Room at Kew, the Society of Genealogists and at various other archives and libraries. Calendars to 1946 are also available at Ancestry although they are not complete.

There are also thirteen district registries across England and Wales, who have calendars going back fifty years as well as copies of wills proved locally.

LETTERS OF ADMINISTRATION

An administration is a legal arrangement which enables the estate of someone who died intestate (that is without making a will) to be wound up. Under such circumstances, it is usual for an adult next of kin (frequently the spouse) to apply to the probate court for a grant, or letters, of administration, usually abbreviated to Admons. Before 1815 grants were normally only applied for if large sums of money were involved and the family could not come to an amicable private arrangement. The records are normally rather disappointing as they often only give name and address of the deceased and the person to whom the admon was granted. Death duty registers give the names of most admons and who benefited from them.

Chapter 7

MILITARY RECORDS BEFORE 1914

Although the numbers of men in Britain's armed forces historically was always small, they played a far greater role in the nation's Imperial rise then their size would have warranted. And for family historians, having soldiers and sailors in the family tree is a bonus because there may well be detailed records about their career in the forces, records which do not exist for men in civilian occupations. These registers, volumes and files were generally kept for two purposes – in order to ensure that pay and pensions were being paid and to keep a record of any disciplinary offences committed.

The British Army

A few regiments in the British Army can trace their origins back to the decades after the restoration of Charles II in 1660. Initially regiments were raised and disbanded as and when they were needed. From the mid-eighteenth century this practice ceased and the Army as a whole became a permanent force. There were further reforms after the Crimean War and particularly in the 1880s which gave the Army its organisational structure for nearly eighty years.

The Army was (and remains) divided into specialist corps such as the Royal Artillery and Royal Engineers, and infantry regiments who engaged in combat with the enemy. From 1881 these regiments often had strong links to particular counties and cities, which were generally reflected in their names.

Infantry regiments are comprised of one or more battalions. Traditionally, one of these battalions was stationed in the Empire, especially India, while the other one was training and recruiting at home. For ordinary soldiers and junior officers life centred on the regiment which provided accommodation and food, discipline and comradeship.

Battalions and cavalry regiments were split into companies, generally made up of 100 men under a captain or major and subdivided into platoons (squadrons in the cavalry), under a lieutenant or second lieutenant (with the assistance of a sergeant) and section of perhaps half a dozen men led by a corporal or lance corporal.

Members of the 2nd battalion South Wales Borderers in the 1880s. Author's collection

Examples of uniforms worn by officers in the 1880s. Author's collection

The Army is composed of officers (such as majors, captains or lieutenants) holding commissions from the Crown, non-commissioned officers (sergeant majors, sergeants, corporals), and ordinary soldiers (privates, riflemen, sappers, gunners). Officers were always in a small minority: fewer than 10 per cent of the strength of the Army were made up of officers.

There was little interaction between officers and the other ranks. Officers almost always were from the upper and middle classes and it was most unusual for men to be promoted from the ranks. Conversely ordinary soldiers often came from the poorest social classes – "the dregs of the earth" in the Duke of Wellington's famous words. The period of enlistment for soldiers varied during the nineteenth century. Initially it was for twenty-one years, in effect for life that is until the soldier was too worn out to continue in the service, or had been wounded in battle.

The vast majority of records you'll need to consult while researching your soldier ancestors are at The National Archives. For officers in particular, regimental museums or archives may well have additional material.

In general the survival of records is pretty good. Where a record is missing it is often possible to find an alternative source which is almost as informative.

Service records

Officers

There is often much to discover about an individual army officer's career, unfortunately however, the records are scattered and can be quite confusing.

The War Office did not begin to keep records of individual officers' service until 1793. Not all records survive. The majority are at Kew, although duplicates can often be found at regimental archives or museums.

Published Army Lists, which begin in the 1740s, will give a basic outline of an individual officer's career. You can follow through from year to year to see promotions, units served in and location. There is a set on the open shelves at The National Archives. Some large libraries may have incomplete runs. They have also been filmed by the LDS church and so are available through Family History Centres. Few Army Lists are available online, although Ancestry, FamilyRelatives, The Genealogist and Findmypast have small collections. In addition S&N Genealogical Supplies has published many Army (and Navy) lists on CD. Details at www.britishdataarchive.com.

Also worth looking out for is *Hart's Army List* published between 1839 and 1915, which includes short biographies of officers. The *London Gazette* also

179

BENGAL.

Seventy-Fourth Regiment Native Infantry.

Station—*Cawnpore. Arrived* , 185 .

Ordered to *Delhi.*

Seav. of Appt.	Names.	Rank in the Regiment.	Army.	Remarks.
	COLONEL.		[L.G.	
1798	I. Truscott	4Mar.830	11Nov 851	On furlough
	LIEUT.-COLONEL.			
1811	J. C. C. Gray	27Aug.847	C28Nv854	Oude irr. force
	MAJOR.			
1831	H. E. S. Abbott	11Nov.854		
	CAPTAINS.			
—	Sir Geo. Parker, Bt.	3 Oct.845	M6Dec. 56	Civil employ
1835	Charles Gordon	15Dec.847		
1836	George Ryley	16Mar.848		
1837	J.P.P.T.Hawkey	1Dec.		
1838	W. F. N.Wallace	1 Feb.849		
1841	J.W. B. Blagrave	11Nov.854		Rev. survey
—	A. G.Nedham	23 do 856	12Jan. 856	2d in com. 11th [ir. cav.
	LIEUTENANTS.			
1842	Fran. J. Burgess	21Dec.844		Rev. surv. dept.
—	G. H. M. Mason	3 Oct 845		Civ.emp. [gen.
1843	G. S. Macbean	15Dec. 847		Sub. asst. com.
—	Hugh Grant	16Mar.848		
1844	H. A. Taylor	1Dec.		
	Wm. H. Lance			
1845	W. C. R. Mylne	1 Feb.849		On furlough
1647	M. H. Reveley	2Aug.851		Do
—	Jas. D. Smith	17 do 853		
1848	Hn.H.R.Addington	11Nov.854		
1849	H. F. M. Hyslop	23 do 856 do		
	ENSIGNS.			
1853	A. P. Mew	12Jan.854	13July853	
1854	H. Sconce	16Aug.	20Feb.854	
1855	R. W. Elton	25 Mar856	8Dec.855	
	..			

Adjutant ··········H. A. Taylor

Inter. and qr.-mas...J.D. Smith   10 Jan. 854

Surgeon ··········S. H. Batson   25 Apr. 853

Assist. do··········   2 Jan. 856

Facines Yellow.

A page from an Army List issued at the time of the Crimean War. The owner has carefully annotated it showing officers who died during the war. Author's collection

records the appointment and promotion of officers and is available online at www.gazettes-online.co.uk, however the indexing here is not very good.

The majority of surviving records are in series WO 76 at The National Archives. There is a card index to the records in the Open Reading Room at Kew, details from which are being added to the online catalogue at the time of writing. Also worth looking at is series WO 25. If your ancestor was commissioned before 1871, then the Commander in Chief's Memoranda in series WO 31 will have papers and correspondence about his background and the purchase of sale of any commissions (as promotion was largely by the purchase of commissions). They are arranged by date of commission, which is given in the Army Lists.

Officers were not entitled to a pension until 1871. Before then, officers wishing to retire sold their commissions or went on half pay. Half pay became a retaining fee paid to the officer, so he was still (in theory) available for future service. Officers on half pay can be traced in the British Army Lists, which gives date of commencement of half pay and occasionally other details as well. There are also records at Kew, particular ledgers of payment, 1737–1921, in PMG 4.

Other ranks

The service records of Other Ranks are fairly easy to find and use. The place to start are the soldiers' documents in series WO 97 at The National Archives. However they only survive for men who received a pension. There are no equivalent records for men who died or were killed while in the Army or had deserted.

The records will tell you:

- When he enlisted and was discharged
- Where he enlisted, place and date of birth and civilian occupation
- A brief personal description with height, hair and eye colour (for some reason almost always brown) and any physical marks or tattoos
- Reasons for discharge – generally either as the result of lingering wounds or ailments (particularly rheumatism) or being 'worn out'
- Provide details of promotions and demotions (generally for drunkenness)
- Where he served
- Details of wife and children (generally in the more recent documents)

SHORT SERVICE.

Army Form B. 265.

ATTESTATION OF

No. *2931* Name *Richard Cavendish*

Corps *4th Hussars*

Joined at *Aldershot*

on *22d July 1882*

Questions to be put to the Recruit before enlistment.

1. What is your Name?	1.	*Richard Cavendish*
2. In or near what Parish or Town were you born?	2. In the Parish of *Clapham*, in or near the Town of *London* in the County of *Middlesex*	
3. What is your Age?	3. *24* Years. ...... Months.	
4. What is your Trade or Calling?	4. *Clerk*	
5. Are you, or have you been, an Apprentice? if so, where? to whom? and for what period?	5. *No*	
6. Have you resided out of your Father's house for three years continuously in the same place, or occupied a house or land of the yearly value of £10 for one year, and paid rates for the same, and, in either case, if so, state where?	6. *No*	
7. Are you Married?	7. *No*	
8. Have you ever been discharged from any part of Her Majesty's Forces, with Ignominy, or as Incorrigible and Worthless, or on account of conviction of felony, or of a sentence of penal servitude, or have you been dismissed with disgrace from the Navy? And have you are warned that there is a special provision in the Army Act which renders you liable to Penal Servitude if you make a false answer to this question.	8. *No*	
9. Do you now belong to, or have you ever served in, Her Majesty's Army?	9. *No*	
10. Do you now belong to, or have you ever served in, the Marines?	10. *No*	
11. Do you now belong to, or have you ever served in, the Militia, or Militia Reserve?	11. *No*	
12. Do you now belong to, or have you ever served in, the Royal Navy?	12. *No*	
13. Do you now belong to the Volunteers, or to the Naval Artillery Volunteers? or to the Royal Naval Reserve Force?	13. *No*	
If so, the Recruit is to be asked the particulars of his former Service, and the cause of his Discharge, and is to produce, if possible, his Parchment Certificate of Discharge.		
14. Have you truly stated the whole, if any, of your previous Service?	14. *Yes*	
15. Have you ever been rejected as unfit for Her Majesty's Service?	15. *No*	
16. For what Corps are you willing to be enlisted, or are you willing to be enlisted for General Service?	16. For *4th Hussars*	
17. Did you receive a Notice, and do you understand its meaning?	17. *Yes*	
18. Who gave you the Notice?	18. *R.J.W. Wilks 4th Hussars*	
19. Are you willing to serve for the term of twelve Years, provided Her Majesty should so long require your services, for the first seven years in Army Service, and for the remaining five years in the 1st Class of the Army Reserve, or if, at the termination of each period of Army Service, you are serving beyond the seas, then for the first eight years in Army Service, and for the remaining four years in the 1st Class of Army Reserve?	19. *Yes*	
20. Are you aware that, at the expiration of the above-mentioned terms of Army Service, whether of seven or eight years, a state of war exists, you will be liable, if so directed by the competent Military Authority, to serve in Army Service for a further term not exceeding 12 months?	20. *Yes*	
21. Are you aware that if, at the expiration of the above-mentioned terms of Army Service, you are so required by a proclamation from Her Majesty in case of imminent national danger or great emergency, you may be required to serve in Army Service so as to complete your term of 12 years, and for a further period not exceeding 12 months?	21. *Yes*	
22. Are you aware that, if the above-mentioned term of 12 years expires while you are on service with the Regular Forces beyond the seas, or while a state of war exists with a Foreign Power, or while soldiers in the Reserve are required by proclamation to continue in or re-enter upon Army Service, you will be liable to serve for a further period not exceeding twelve months?	22. *Yes*	

I, *Richard Cavendish*, do solemnly declare that the above answers made by me to the above questions are true and that I am willing to fulfil the engagement made.

Richard Cavendish Signature of Recruit *J. Renshew* Signature of Witness

OATH TO BE TAKEN BY RECRUIT ON ATTESTATION.

I, *Richard Cavendish*, do make Oath, that I will be faithful and bear true Allegiance to Her Majesty, Her Heirs, and Successors, and that I will, as in duty bound, honestly and faithfully defend Her Majesty, Her Heirs, and Successors, in Person, Crown, and Dignity, against all enemies, and will observe and obey all orders of Her Majesty, Her Heirs, and Successors, and of the Generals and Officers set over me. So help me God.

Witness my hand. Signature of Recruit *Richard Cavendish*

Signature of Witness *J. Renshew*

CERTIFICATE OF MAGISTRATE.

The Recruit above-named was cautioned by me that if he made any false answer to any of the above questions he would be liable to be punished as provided in the Army Act.

The above questions were then read to the recruit in my presence.

I have taken care that he understands each question, and that his answer to each question has been duly entered as replied to, and the said recruit has made and signed the declaration and oath before me at *Aldershot* on this *22nd* day of *July* 1882.

Signature of the Justice

The Recruit should, if he requires it, receive a copy of the ....

Soldiers' documents for Richard Cavendish. TNA WO 97/2478 (FindMyPast)

A cartes de visite of Richard Cavendish. He was supposed to have the illegitimate son of the King of Prussia. While in the Army he rose rapidly through the ranks, but left after his term of service expired. Richard later became master of Langport Workhouse in Somerset. James Cavendish

350 OXFORD RO/
MANCHESTER

These records can be seen on online at www.findmypast.co.uk or at Kew. A few records are at www.nationalarchives.gov.uk/documentsonline. Brief details of soldiers between 1760 and 1854 can be found in The National Archives' catalogue.

But not everything is in WO 97: service records for men in the Royal Artillery, 1791–1863, are in WO 54 (as well as Royal Engineers) and WO 69, and records for men who served in the Household Cavalry are in WO 400 (1791–1920).

If you can't find your man in WO 97, particularly before 1854, it is worth checking out series WO 121 and WO 119, which include many service records of men who applied to Chelsea and Kilmainham hospitals respectively for a pension. These records will be put online by Findmypast in due course.

If you can't find a service record there are a number of other places to try, including:

- Muster rolls, provide a monthly account of everybody in the battalion, with details of pay and where they were serving (series WO 12–16)
- Description books provide physical descriptions of individual soldiers, which would have been used to track him had he deserted (WO 25)
- If he left the army in the decade before 1914 his records may be with the WW1 service records (see below)
- Soldiers and their families, no matter where they were serving, are included in the 1911 census (see Chapter 5)

Pensions were awarded by Chelsea Royal Hospital. The famous pensioners in their red uniforms, known as in-pensioners, made only a small number of the men helped by the Hospital. Surviving records for out-pensioners, that is men who were not resident in Chelsea are at The National Archives largely in series WO 116 and WO 117. Admission papers for in-pensioners are in WO 23.

Casualties

There are no central records of men who were killed in battle before the First World War (see below). There are however a number of casualty rolls, which usually give date of death and unit of the man who died, the originals are often at The National Archives, but many have been printed. A number from the 1870s onwards are at www.britishmedals.us/kevin/intro.html. Those for the Boer War (1899–1902) are at www.ancestors.co.uk

Medals

There are three types of medals:

- Gallantry-awarded for bravery in battle. The most famous of these medals is of course the Victoria Cross. Citations (that is a description of the action for which the medal was awarded) are often but not always published in the *London Gazette* (all online at www.gazettes-online.co.uk)
- Campaign medals – awarded for service in a particular campaign or war. Names are published in medal rolls, which are at The National Archives in series WO 100. Generally only men who survived received a medal.

Examples of the Queen's and King's South African medals awarded to soldiers who served in the Boer War. The bars on the medals indicate the various actions the soldier took part in.
John Sly

There is no central list of names so you will need to know the campaign and the regiment in which the individual served. Few medal rolls are yet online (but check out www.britishmedals.us/kevin/intro.html) but many have been published. However the Waterloo Medal, issued to men still alive in 1848 who had fought at the battle in 1815, is online at www.findmypast.com, www.military-genealogy.com and www.national archives.gov.uk/documentsonline.

- Long service and good conduct medals – as the name suggests these basically were awarded for keeping "your nose clean". Rolls are at The National Archives in series WO 101 and WO 102

There are several excellent introductions to medals and how to use them in your research including:

The Medals Yearbook (Token Publishing annually)
Peter Duckers, *British Military Medals: a guide for collectors and family historians* (Pen & Sword, 2009)
William Spencer, *Medals: The Researchers' Guide* (The National Archives, 2007)

There are fewer equivalent websites, but www.britishmedals.info is worth looking at. As always Wikipedia has brief pages about individual British medals.

Campaign records

It is difficult to find very much in the records about individual battles or actions that an ancestor fought in without considerable difficulty. The best place to start are the plethora of books on the various wars and campaigns that the British Army were engaged in (those by Richard Holmes and Byron Farwell are especially good). Of more specialist interest are regimental histories which provide a more detailed account of the actions that individual battalions took part in. There are an increasing number of websites, although the quality does vary – many are listed in my *Internet Research for Military Historians* (Pen & Sword, 2007). A reliable starting point is Wikipedia: entries often provide links to other websites.

PART-TIME SOLDIERS

There have also been a number of men who were part-time officers and soldiers and could be called to serve in case of national emergency. They served in a wide range of units, generally with the title of militia (infantry) or yeomanry (cavalry). Records are largely at local record offices. Such militias go back to Saxon times, but most records survive from the 1750s onwards.

In the late nineteenth century young men would join their local militia unit before enlisting in the professional Army, so they are worth checking out. A series of militia attestation papers from 1806 to 1915 is in series WO 96, although you need to know the regiment. Most of the attestations however are from the later period. Part of the series has been indexed (1886–1910) and online at www.originsnetwork.com.

Further reading:
Byron Farwell, *For Queen and Country: a social history of the Victorian and Edwardian Army* (Viking, 1981)
Simon Fowler, *Tracing Your Army Ancestors* (Pen & Sword, 2006)
Richard Holmes, *Redcoat: the British soldier in the age of the horse and musket* (HarperCollins, 2001)
William Spencer, *Army Ancestors* (The National Archives, 2008)

The Royal Navy

Until the 1850s, when a permanent career structure was introduced, ratings (that is ordinary seamen) signed on for a particular voyage, so might well serve on both Royal Navy and merchant ships. And officers might spend much of their time ashore on half pay, waiting for a posting.

It is fair to say that naval vessels had changed little so that a sailor who had fought against the Spanish Amada in 1588, would have noticed little difference at the Battle of Trafalgar except that the ships were much bigger. This would change during the nineteenth century the Navy's equipment and tactics were revolutionised: steam replaced wind-power, the screw propeller supplanted the sail, bigger and better guns were introduced, and wireless telegraphy transformed how ships communicated.

Conditions for ratings also slowly improved. Under Nelson, standard rations were based on hard ship's biscuits, salt beef and pork, all of which could be years old, although breakfast consisted of a mixture of oatmeal and molasses, known as 'burgoo'. Fresh vegetables and fruit were provided, to counteract scurvy, but could be hard to come by on long missions in foreign waters. By the First World War conditions had considerably improved – larger ships for example might have even their own bakeries.

One thing which did not change was the system of messing, where by small groups of men, from the same branch (or specialism) ate, lived and socialised together in messes. Officers too had their own messes. The Navy had many different specialist branches, such as writers (ie clerks), seamen, stokers and sailmakers

Personnel records are at The National Archives, although there are many other sources of records, particularly the Fleet Air Arm Museum, National Maritime Museum, and the Royal Naval Museum. Excellent information sheets on the history of the Navy are at www.royalnavalmuseum.org/research_info_sheets.htm

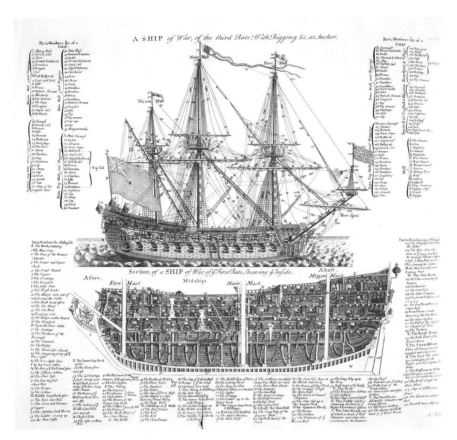

A diagram of a third class Man of War about 1728 showing how complex such a vessel was.
Cycloedpia of War (1728)

Service records

Naval service records are not as informative as their Army counterparts. However, you should discover:

- The ships a man served on
- A brief note of conduct, generally g (good) or vg (very good)
- Promotions
- Personal details including date of discharge (if 'run' this indicates that he had deserted) and details of when he enlisted and next of kin

Most pre-1920 service records have been indexed and digitised and are available online at www.nationalarchives.gov.uk/documentsonline.

For general advice about research into RN officers and seamen www.mariners-l.co.uk is a good bet. There are also pages about shore stations (which confusingly to non-mariners are given ships' names) and where they were located and a history of the Royal Naval School at Greenwich. A few examples of transcripts of individuals' service records (mainly for the late nineteenth century Navy) are at www.rimell.u-net.com

Officers

Although there were commissioned officers and ratings the divide between the led and their leaders was not so clear-cut as it was in the Army. Beneath officers were warrant officers – a very disparate group; some of whom were 'sea officers' and some were only 'inferior officers'. In the eighteenth century, Warrant sea officers were the heads of specialised branches of the ships company, they included the Master, the Surgeon, the Purser, the Boatswain, the Gunner and the Carpenter. The inferior warrant officers were the Cook, Chaplain, Armourer, Schoolmaster, Master at Arms and Sailmaker. Over the next century many of the warrant officers were transferred to commissioned rank. By the 1860s warrant officers now only included Boatswains, Gunners, Carpenters, Sailmakers and Masters-at-Arms. For more about this consult NAM Rodger, *Naval Records for Genealogists* (Public Record Office, 1998).

The starting point for research is through the official Navy List, which lists all officers, the branches they served with and promotions. It has been published since 1814. A complete set is on the shelves at Kew and in specialist naval museums. In addition the Family History Library has copies on microfilm which can be ordered from any LDS Family History Centre. The Navy List contains a great deal of information on officers and is the best and natural starting point.

There is one main series of records at The National Archives: ADM 196. Although the series covers the period between 1777 and 1931, systematic record keeping did not really start until the 1840s, so you may not find your officer here. There are entries for both commissioned officers and warrant officers. The records are available online at www.nationalarchives.gov.uk/documentsonline.

Also of use are the pay lists in series ADM 24 between 1795 and 1905, which record payments to commissioned officers who were actively employed. They normally give only the officer's name and the exact dates of each voyage.

If you are looking for officers before 1814 then *Commissioned Sea Officers of the Royal Navy 1660–1815* may help. A copy is at www.ancestry.co.uk: other providers may also have copies. Another website www.pbenyon1.plus.com is an attractive miscellanea of a site generally reprinting pages from newspapers and books, with lots of names, particularly of officers. It is also simply laid out and there are lists of officers between 1844 and 1879 taken from the Navy Lists.

There are various series of records for officers on half pay (that is payments to officers who had retired but who could theoretically be recalled if needed) or in receipt of a superannuation pension.

Other Ranks

There are no service records for ratings until 1853. Men were discharged at the end of each voyage so there is no continuity of service. There are however several places which might provide information:

- For men who retired with a pension between 1802 and 1894, are the certificates of service, which list the ships served on and dates of service. The records are being indexed and the indexes placed in The National Archives' online catalogue;
- Ships' muster and pay books which will tell you when he enlisted, his age and place of birth
- Ships' logbooks can also help on occasion and certainly provide more information on the voyages themselves such as weather and navigational details
- A small collection of seamen's wills are available on Documents Online. Also worth checking out are the wills in the Prerogative Court of Canterbury (also on Documents Online) – for more details see chapter 6 above;
- Details of men who served at the Battle of Trafalgar in October 1805 are in the Trafalgar Ancestors Database at www.nationalarchives.gov.uk/ trafalgarancestors

After 1853 Continuous Service Engagement Books contain brief records for each rating. They are all online through Documents Online – www.national

204459 *Chatham* 204459

Name in full } John Richard Lyon

Date of Birth 20 January 1884
Place of Birth Liverpool, Lancs.
Occupation Labourer

Date and Period of C. S. Engagements.	Age.	Height. Ft. in.	Hair.	Eyes.	Complexion.	Wounds, Scars, Marks, &c.
20 January 1902 – 12 yrs	26 18	4.11¾ 5.2	Dk brn	brn	fresh	Crossed hands + arm

Ships, &c., served in.	List and No.	Rating.	Sub-ratings. Rating. From To	Badges.	Period of Service. From To	Character.	If Discharged, Whither, and for what Cause.
Caledonia	156 w451	B 2 c B 1 c	2m 30ct 04		19 May 99		
Minotaur	15c 3391	"			22 Feb 00 26 Apl 00		
Agincourt	15c 1183	"			27 Apl 00 18 Sep 00	V.G.	
Sans Pareil	5 1137	"			19 Sep 00 28 Oct 00		
					29 Oct 00 31 Dec 01		
Grafton	5 202	Ord.			1 Jan 02 13 Jan 02		
					14 Jan 02	V.G.	
	"	A.B.			1 Jan 02 to man o3	N.E. 31.12.03 as above bills	
					1 Apl 03	Good 31.12.03	
					30 Apl 03 23 Sep 04	Good.	D.D. 23 Sep 04 Drowned at Sheerness in attempting to cross the Harbour in a canoe Body since recovered
							N.L. 13103 / 04

Class for Conduct.

2nd 21.303 1st 2.10.03

Clothing and Bedding Gratuities.		REMARKS.	
£ G.P. June 99			
2.5.6. Sep 99			
£ G. uch 00			
£3.6. Sep 00.			

A Continuous Engagement Service record for Seaman John Richard Lyon who died in a canoeing accident in Sheerness Harbour in September 1904 aged just 20. TNA ADM 188/355 archives.gov.uk/documentsonline, where you can download individual service records for a fee.

The records will tell you:

- When and where a man enlisted and his date and place of birth
- Ships served on (including shore establishments)
- Promotions
- Conduct (generally g for good or vg for very good) while onboard
- Discipline (often a brief note about the offence and the punishment meted out)
- Medals awarded, particularly those for long service and good conduct
- Date of discharge and reason. Usually this was because the man had completed his term of enlistment, but death in service will be noted

As with officers there are several series of pension records paid by the Royal Greenwich Hospital and its successors mostly in series ADM 29 and ADM 73.

Casualty records

There is no central list of men who died while serving in the Royal Navy, although series ADM 104 has details of men who died at sea from 1893 onwards. Deaths should however be recorded on the ship's muster and pay lists. Captain's logs may also include the names of men who died on board.

Medals

Rolls are in series ADM 171 at The National Archives. They are not arranged by name, so you need to know the date when the medal was awarded and the ship your ancestor served on or station (base) where the award was made.

Operational records

It is difficult to find out much about what an ancestor did in the Navy, ship's logs at The National Archives generally only record weather and navigational details. An increasing number of these logs are available at www.national archives.gov.uk/documentsonline.

Potentially of more use is the Admiralty correspondence in series ADM 1, which include letters and reports from ships' captains and much else besides. However you need to use the original registers of correspondence (ADM 12) to track down what you want, which are not easy to use as well as being very heavy to lift. You can find further suggestions in two TNA in depth research guides: *Royal Navy: Operational Records 1660–1914* and *Royal Navy: Log Books and Reports of Proceedings*. Probably of more immediate use are websites, such as Wikipedia (which may have brief histories of individual ships), www.battleships-cruisers.co.uk and for photographs www.navyphotos.co.uk.

Lists of men on board Royal Naval ships can be found in the 1861, 1901 and 1911 censuses. An index to RN ships in the 1901 census is at http://homepage.ntlworld.com/jeffery.knaggs/RNShips.htmls.

Further reading:
Roy and Lesley Adkins, *Jack Tar: life in Nelson's Navy* (Abacus, 2009)
Bruno Pappalardo, *Tracing Your Naval Ancestors* (The National Archives, 2003)
NAM Rodger, *The Wooden Wall* (Collins, 1986)

THE ROYAL MARINES

Initially founded in the 1755 to act as "sea soldiers", the Royal Marines are (and remain) somewhat an anomaly. They are part of the Royal Navy, but largely have Army ranks and indeed have their antecedents as an Army regiment which was initially formed in 1664. Only since the Second World War have they had their commando role, initially they were used to enforce discipline on board ship, manned one or more of the gun turrets and also were sent ashore to protect naval landing parties.

Traditionally the Marines were divided into three divisions: Chatham, Portsmouth and Plymouth (with a short-lived one at Woolwich during the first half of the nineteenth century). During the nineteenth century the Marines were split into the Royal Marine Light Infantry (sometimes known as the Red Marines, from the colour of their uniform) and Royal Marine Artillery (the Blue Marines). They were reunited in 1923.

Service records for both officers and other ranks are largely available at Documents Online. Not yet online are attestation papers for Marines (ADM 157) which will be useful if you are researching a marine who served between 1790 and 1842 when service records begin.

Further reading:
Richard Brookes and Matthew Taylor, *Tracing Royal Marine Ancestors* (Pen & Sword, 2008)
Ken Divall, *My Ancestors was a Royal Marine* (Society of Genealogists, 2008)

Name William Wing Walden **Register No.** 4253 **Division** Chatham

Date of Birth	27 Oct. 1874	When re-engaged		Father David
Where Born	Harlow Kingston on Thames	Name of Kin and their address		of Sunbury Lane
Trade	C.H.E.			Walton on Thames
Religion				
When enlisted	27 Feb. 1893			
Where enlisted	London			

DESCRIPTION OF PERSON.

For Drummer ⸱ On Enlistment as a Boy
only. ⸱ On Attaining the age of 18
On Enlistment as Private
On Re-engagement
On Final Discharge from the Service

Feet	In.	Complexion	Hair	Eyes	Marks, Wounds, and Scars
5	6½	Fresh	D. Brn	Blue	Nil

Rank	On	Name of Division or Ship	No. on Ship's Books	Entry	Discharge	Cause of Discharge from Division or Ship	Character	Ability	Recommended for Medal and Gratuity	Name of Commanding Officer
Pte		H.M. Depot Walmer		27 Feb 93	5 Oct 93	td - to td batt	Good	Good		Jno Scott
		Chatham Dn.		6 Oct 93	31 Dec 93		V.G	V.G		Aug. Grange
		Do.	4734	1 Jan 94	14 July 94	Embarked	V.G	V.G		Aug. Grange
		Camperdown		15 July 94	31 Dec 94		V.G	Good		Aug. Grange
		Do.		1 Jan 95	31 Dec 95		Good	Good		Aug. Grange
		Do.		1 Jan 96	31 Dec 96					
		Do.		1 Jan 97	12 May 97	Ld. Gro on passage	V.G	V.G		H.G. Bird
		Chatham Dn		13 May 97	6 Nov 97		V.G	V.G		H.G. Bird
		Do.		7 Nov 97	31 Dec 97					
				1 Jan 98	14 Oct 98	Embarked				
		Icarus		15 Oct 98	8 Dec 98	D.D.	V.G	V.G		H.G. Bird

Drowned through falling from the Pier at Cromer

4746. James Seymour

Pte		Wallaroo	14 Apr	Jan 95	31 Dec 15		V.G	Sgt		R.M. West
		Do.		Jan 16	30 Apr 16					
		Chatham		2 May 16	3 Dec 16	Emb td			Bmbr RMA	
		Pembroke		3 Dec 16	28 Dec 16	Speech Lieut RMA				
		President David		29 Dec 16	31 Dec 16		V.G	Sgt		W.R. Kee
				1 Jan 17	31 Dec 17		V.G	Sgt		H. Wilson
				1 Jan 18	31 Dec 18		V.G	Sgt		Guy Livingstone
				1 Jan 19	27 Feb 19					
		Chatham Div		24 Feb 19	8 Apr 19	Demob bisd	V.G	Sgt		H.W Graham

address 6 East Terrace South Queensferry N.B.

Re-enrolled in R.F. Reserve 8 March 1919
Re-enrolled on Engagement 23 April 1920
Chatham Dn (on Mobilisation) demobilised
10 Sep. 1921 Paid R.F.R. Gratuity

SERVICES FORFEITED.

SERVICES RESTORED.

| | | | |
DATES OF PASSING AND REVISION OF DRILLS.

	Class.	Date.	No. in Possession	Date	Rank.	Co.	Date.
	First	27 Feb 93	One	1 Jan 96			
			Nil	6 July 95			
			One	31 Jan 97			

Good Conduct Badges Promotions and Reductions.

Passed for

INVALIDED.

WOUNDS AND HURTS.

SCHOOL CERTIFICATE.

Able to Swim? Yes
When Tested 11.4.93
Where Walmer
When married

Service record for Marine William Walden of the Chatham Division. He died as a result of a fall from the pier at Cromer in December 1898. TNA ADM 159/47

Chapter 8

MILITARY RECORDS FOR THE TWO WORLD WARS

I can almost guarantee that every reader of this book will have an ancestor who fought in one or both of the great world wars of the twentieth century. In my own family, for example, Great Uncle Stanley fought (and died) in Belgium during the Great War – and my maternal grandfather won an Iron Cross while serving with the German Army; two cousins served with the Air Transport Auxiliary during Hitler's War. My wife's paternal grandfather was not conscripted in 1916 because of a tubercular shadow (he lived to the ripe old age of 96) and during the Second World War both her parents were officers in the Royal Army Medical Corps.

There are lots of records available – again mostly at The National Archives – which will allow you to find more about your ancestors' experiences.

The First World War

Nearly six million men served during the First World War (mainly with the Army), of whom 704,000 made the ultimate sacrifice. As a result almost every family had one or more men with the colours. As a result in recent years this has become a very popular research topic.

It is also fairly easy to research individuals as most records are now online. But because of the large number of servicemen with the same name (there were 24,000 John Smiths, for example) it is helpful to know:

• The individual soldier's service number
• The unit he served with

As this will help identify the man you are researching. However, he may have served in several units and, as a result, would have been assigned several service numbers. Normally the unit he was serving with at time of death or discharge is the one that appears in the records. These details should be on any medals that you have inherited or in old photographs: you may be able

A photograph of my Great-Uncle Stanley Crozier who was killed in action in October 1918.
Adrian Lead

to identify a unit from badges on caps or buttons. And of course there may be family stories about his service which can supply valuable clues.

There are several websites which can help you identify regimental badges. A favourite, based on the carvings found on war graves, is at www.ww1 cemeteries.com/regimentalarchive/regimental_archive_mainpage.htm

You also need to be aware that only roughly a third of service records for ordinary soldiers survive. Most records were lost in a fire in 1940, which explains why many of the documents either look singed or water-damaged. This is a blow, but not fatal as there are other records which will fill in the gaps.

Medal Index Cards

The most important series of records are the Medal Index Cards, which will give you brief information about your soldier. These Cards record the award of campaign medals to all men (and a small number of women) who served overseas from August 1914 to November 1918 to men in the Army and the Royal Air Force. Other ranks were sent the medals automatically, but officers had to claim theirs.

The medals on the card are:

- British War Medal, awarded to all service personnel who saw service overseas.
- Victory Medal, also awarded to all service personnel who saw service overseas
- 1914 Star (sometimes erroneously called the Mons Star), awarded to men who saw action in France and Flanders between 4 August-22 November 1914
- 1914–15 Star, awarded to men who served in France and Flanders between 4 August 1914 and 31 December 1915
- Silver War Badge, awarded to soldiers who had been honourably discharged because of wounds
- Territorial Force War Medal, for men who had previously served in the Territorial Army

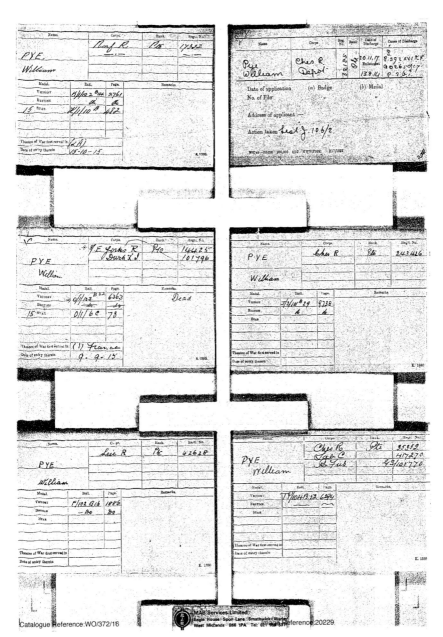

Please note correct medal card is the left hand one in the middle row.

Catalogue Reference:WO/372/16

The Cards will give you:

- Name
- Unit(s)
- Regiment al number(s)
- Medals awarded
- Roll on which the award has been recorded

Occasionally other information is given, such as:

- Date arrived overseas
- Theatre of operations where he served (normally "France and Belgium") – this is often abbreviated, ie 1a is for France and Belgium
- Date of death
- Home address (occasionally found on the rear of the card)

The cards are available online in two places:

- www.ancestry.co.uk (called Medal Rolls Index)
- www.nationalarchives.gov.uk/documentsoneline

Ancestry's set is available as part of their subscription package. They have been filmed in colour and include the backs where appropriate. However, the indexing is not as good as it could be. Cards on Documents Online cost £2 each to download. They are filmed in black and white (which is surprisingly hard to read). Documents Online also include cards for medals awarded to civilian personnel (such as charity workers) who went overseas. In addition their indexing is rather superior.

If you are interested you can check out the rolls for which these cards were the index. The only additional information you will find is the battalion in which the individual served. The rolls are in series WO 329 at The National Archives.

Service records

Army

First World War service records are some of the most popular records at Kew – little wonder because they can contain information it is impossible to find elsewhere. But nearly two-thirds of those for other ranks have been lost. There appears to be no rhyme or reason to what survives or has been destroyed.

Officers

Officers are listed in the *Army Lists*, which were published quarterly during the war. For intelligence reasons the information given is not as comprehensive as in peacetime lists. Even so it should be possible to track down promotions and the date they were made. The National Archives has a complete set on the open shelves in the Open Reading Room.

Some 271,800 officers' service records are with The National Archives, perhaps 85% of the total. They are not yet online, so you will need to visit Kew to read them.

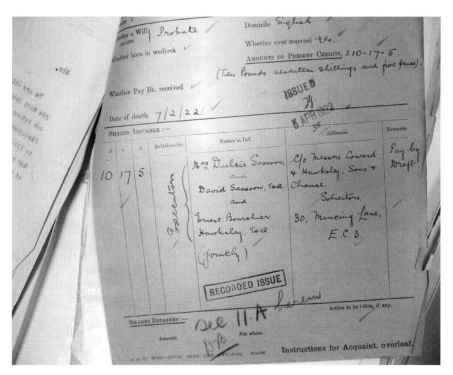

A page from an officers' service record. TNA WD374/60413

What survives is a duplicate series of folders, generally containing correspondence about a man's death, or pension eligibility, rather than about an individual's war service.

Other ranks
Where they survive, service records may tell you:

- When and where a man enlisted
- Date and place of discharge
- Personal details including height, colour of eyes, and occupation in civilian life
- Promotions
- Disciplinary offences
- Medical treatment

There may also be correspondence about pension, medal claims or relatives seeking a missing man. The records will not say very much about the action he saw, for this you will need the war diaries (see below).

The records are online at www.ancestry.co.uk/ww1. Here they are divided into service and pension records. However, many users have grumbled about the poor indexing. It is also possible to order microfilm to be read at LDS Family History Centres for a small fee.

They are arranged in strict alphabetical order by surname and then by forename. You should know in which unit a man served and his regimental number, particularly for men with common names. There are also a small numbers of miscellaneous files found during filming which can be found at the end of each series.

There are three series of service records:

The 'burnt' records (or 'service records' on Ancestry), as they were damaged in someway by fire or water in 1940. These service records relate to soldiers: who were:

- Killed in action
- Died of wounds or disease without being discharged to pension
- Demobilised at the end of the war

The 'unburnt' records ('pension records'), because they were either untouched by the fire or subsequently added from other sources. They relate to:

The service record for William Pye is very informative. It reveals that he was disciplined for being absent without leave and that he spent much of 1917 and 1918 working in the regimental office back in Britain. He returned to France in June 1918. The National Archives (Ancestry)

> **OTHER SOURCES**
>
> If you ancestor stayed in the Army after the end of 1920 for other ranks, or April 1922 for officers, then his service record will be with the Ministry of Defence's Army Personnel Centre, Historic Disclosures, Mailpoint 555, Kentigern House, 65 Brown St, Glasgow G2 8EX, www.veterans-uk.info.
>
> Records of Guardsmen and their officers are still with the Guards Museum, Wellington Barracks, Birdcage Walk, London SW1E 6HQ.
>
> An interesting but incomplete source is the fourteen volumes of *National Roll of Honour*, which was published in the years after the war. It comprised short biographical description of some 100,000 individuals, both men and women, civilians as well as servicemen. It is online at www.findmypast.co.uk. The Society of Genealogists has a set of the original volumes.

- Regular soldiers discharged at the end of their period of service. Men who signed up for the duration of the war got a gratuity on demobilisation, and will not be found here unless they received a pension on medical grounds.
- Men discharged on medical and associated grounds, including those who died after the award of a pension

Service records in WO 400 for men of the Household Cavalry, which included the Life Guards, Royal Horse Guards, and Household Battalions are not filmed, so you will need to go to The National Archives to read them. These records are complete.

Royal Air Force

The Royal Air Force (RAF) was formed on 1 April 1918 from the Royal Flying Corps and Royal Naval Air Service. Men who only served with these units can be found in the army and naval records respectively.

Service records are at The National Archives. Officers' records are in series AIR 76 and other ranks in AIR 79. They are for men who left the service before the end of 1922 and 1924 respectively. Later service records are still with the Ministry of Defence – details at www.veterans-uk.info/service_records/raf.html.

The records are not terribly informative, but will give you:

- Units served with
- Promotions
- Date of death or discharge
- A note on conduct and disciplinary offences (if any)
- Next of kin and home address.
- Civilian occupation and date of birth

The officers' records, but not those for other ranks, are online at www.national archives.gov.uk/documentsonline.

Brief details of officers appear in the *Air Force List*. Initially training of pilots was organised by the Royal Aero Club. Records of these men are now on Ancestry.

Royal Navy

Records for both officers and ratings are also online at Documents Online. Again neither are terribly informative. Documents Online also has Royal Marine officer and marine service records.

Officers
Brief details of officers can be found in the published *Navy Lists*.
Service records in ADM 196 will provide:

- Personal details and next of kin
- Promotions and ships served on
- Brief notes about a man's performance

Ratings
Records of ratings are in ADM 188. These records will tell you,

- Which ships and branch a man served with
- Promotions
- Brief remarks about conduct
- Date and place of birth

The Fleet Air Arm Museum (address in Appendix 3) has engagement books for men who joined between 1905 and 1921. These books including details of date and place of joining, physical description, details of any previous military service, and parent's consent if the entrant was a boy.

Royal Naval Reserve (RNR) and Royal Naval Volunteer Reserve (RNVR)
The Royal Navy had several reserve forces from whom men were called up in time of war. The most important of these was the Royal Naval Reserve (RNR) whose men came from merchant ships. Officers' service records are in ADM 240 and they are also mentioned in the *Navy List*. Records of ratings are in BT 377/7.

There was also the Royal Naval Volunteer Reserve (RNVR), whose members came from a much wider range of civilian occupations. Service records for RNVR officers and ratings are in series ADM 337.

Naval personnel were entitled to the same campaign medals as their military counterparts. Rolls for these medals are in ADM 171. They are not yet online.

Unit records

Service records only provide part of the story. To find out what your ancestor did day by day you will need to consult unit records, that is war diaries (Army), Squadron Record Books (RAF) and captains' reports or ships' logs (Royal Navy). With the exception of some war diaries, with Documents Online, none of these records are online or likely to be in the foreseeable future.

War Diaries

These were compiled by infantry or cavalry battalions or equivalent units in the Royal Artillery and other corps. What they include varies tremendously from detailed accounts of battles and skirmishes to reports of football matches and training sessions. Casualties are also noted. Unfortunately it is rare for anybody but an officer to be named. A typical report might say that "Lt Jones and 6OR [other ranks] were killed, 6 OR missing."

The originals are at The National Archives in series WO 95 (an increasing proportion are online through Documents Online) with copies often at regimental museums and archives. War diaries for battalions in the Berkshire

A scene that would have all too familiar to men in the front line. Here a soldier from the Cheshire Regiment keeps look out "Somewhere in France" in 1916. Taylor Collection

and Wiltshire regiments are online at www.thewardrobe.org.uk and a number of other regimental museums and individuals may have also posted extracts from war diaries online.

Squadron Record Books

These are the RAF equivalent to war diaries, but rather more informal. Their survival is rather patchy, but those which do are in series AIR 1 at Kew. Extracts may occasionally be found online.

Royal Navy

It can be frustratingly difficult to track down reports and descriptions of activities during the First World War. Ships' Logs normally only include weather and navigational details. Perhaps of more immediate use are the brief histories of most royal naval ships at www.battleships-cruisers.co.uk/royal.htm. It is also worth checking to see whether there is an entry in Wikipedia.

Otherwise material might be found in three other series at Kew: the online catalogue might be able to assist you in your search. It is best to start with series ADM 137, which contains most of the Admiralty papers for the period. If this is unsuccessful try ADM 116 and then ADM 1.

Casualty records

There are substantial records for the fallen. In many ways it is easier to find more about them then for the men who survived.

Commonwealth War Graves Commission

Established in 1917 to maintain the graves of those who had died and commemorate their lives, the Commonwealth War Graves Commission (CWGC) continues to do this work. And if you are researching a man who was killed during the War you should attempt to visit the cemetery in which he lies as it will be an experience that you will remember forever.

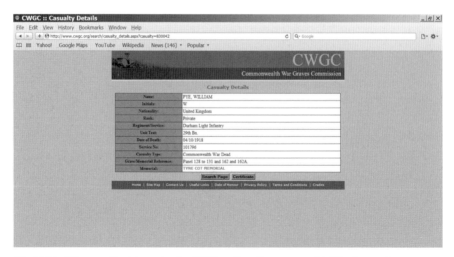

The Debt of Honour Register entry for William Pye. Commonwealth War Graves Commission

Details of individual servicemen can be found in the Debt of Honour register, which is online at www.cwgc.org (or you can write to them at 2 Marlow Road, Maidenhead SL6 7DX for the same information). The Register is easy to use and you will find the following:

- Name
- Regiment, rank and service number
- Cemetery and exact location of grave
- Date of death

In addition many entries include details of the next of kin.

The website also provides details of the cemetery and how to find it. Ancestry has a digitised copy of the original Debt of Honour Register which may occasionally contain more information than can be found on CWGC's own site.

If you are unable to visit the cemetery The War Graves Photographic Project may be able to help. Their aim is to photograph all British and Commonwealth war graves. Many photos are already on their website and they will try to assist enquirers. Details at www.thewargravesproject.org.uk.

Soldiers Died in the Great War

Complementing and on occasion supplementing the information on the Debt of Honour Register are the 81 volumes of "Soldiers Died in the Great War" which was compiled by the War Office in the early 1920s. An entry will give you

- Name
- Regiment, rank and number
- Date of death and cause of death (killed in action, died of wounds or died, ie of sickness)
- Theatre of operations where he died (generally France and Flanders)

Some entries also give extra information, such a man's former regiment, where he enlisted and place of residence (but not a street address).

It is available online at:

- www.ancestry.co.uk
- www.findmypast.co.uk
- www.familyrelatives.com
- www.military-genealogy.com

Many reference libraries have "Soldiers Died" available on CD.

Other sources

Every town and village has a war memorial – there are some 60,000 across the United Kingdom. They are listed by the National Inventory of War Memorials at www.ukniwm.org.uk. There is no national index to the names on memorials. There have, however, been a number of projects researching the men who appear on individual memorials. Two of the best are for Cheltenham – www.remembering.org.uk – and Wolverhampton – www.wolverhamptonwar memorials.org.uk – although a search of the internet will turn up many more, and several hundred are listed in my *Military History on the Internet* (Pen & Sword, 2007).

Hundreds of private rolls of honour were published in the years after the Armistice. Generally they don't provide more than name and regimental details and in the case of company rolls of honour the department or factory where he worked. There is no national collection, although the Imperial War Museum and Society of Genealogists have large numbers. Many are also available online at www.roll-of-honour.com.

Curiously it is possible to get death certificates for the fallen. They can be obtained in the normal way from the General Register Office, although it is not worth it as they do not provide any additional information.

Further reading:
Geoff Bridger, *The Great War Handbook: a guide for family historians and students of the conflict* (Pen & Sword, 2009)
Peter Doyle, *The British Soldier of the First World War* (Shire Books, 2008)
Simon Fowler, *Tracing Your First World War Ancestors* (2nd edition, Countryside Books, 2008)
Richard Holmes, *The Western Front: Ordinary Soldiers and the Defining Battles of World War I* (2nd edition, BBC Books, 2008)
William Spencer, *Family History in the Wars* (The National Archives, 2007)

William Spencer, *First World War Army Service Records* (3rd edition, The
National Archives, 2008)
Richard van Emden, *Britain's Last Tommies* (Pen & Sword, 2005)

In addition there's also a DVD *Tracing Great War Ancestors: Finding Uncle Bill*
(Pen & Sword, 2010) which tells the story of William Pye (with a cameo
appearance by myself).

There are lots of websites devoted to the First World War and retelling the
experiences of the men who fought on the Western Front and elsewhere. It is
worth searching by the regiment or unit that your ancestor served in to see
if there is a website devoted to it. There are a number of general websites, of
which the best is www.1914–1918.net. Also of interest is www.worldwar1.nl
and www.fylde.demon.co.uk/welcome.htm

The Second World War

It is often said that the Second World War is too recent an event for you to be
able to research an ancestor who fought in it. This is not strictly true, although
certain records have not yet been released. However, there is very few
reasons yet online although are masses of websites devoted to individual
units or actions. An excellent introduction to the War and the role of the
British Army is at www.ww2battlefields.info.

Service records

These are with the Ministry of Defence. They are only available to the service
personnel themselves and their direct next of kin (which you have to prove).
MOD may also charge £30 for each one. You can find out more at
www.veterans.info or write to

- Army Personnel Centre, Disclosure 2, Mail Point 515, Kentigern House, 65
  Brown Street, Glasgow G2 8EX
- RAF DPA SAR Section, Room 220, Trenchard Hall, RAF Cranwell, Sleaford
  NG34 8HB
- RN Disclosures Cell, Room 48, West Battery , Whale Island, Portsmouth
  PO2 8DX (also for Royal Marines)

If you are researching an officer the Army, Navy and Air Force Lists will give
you brief details of their career. Copies are available at The National Archives.

The grave of Private Adam Wakenshaw, VC at El Alamein War Graves Cemetery in Egypt. The citation for the award of the medal reads: "On the 27th June, 1942, south of Mersa Matruh, Private Wakenshaw was a member of the crew of a 2-pounder anti-tank gun. An enemy tracked vehicle towing a light gun came within short range. The gun crew opened fire and succeeded in immobilising the enemy vehicle. Another mobile gun came into action, killed or seriously wounded the crew manning the 2-pounder, including Private Wakenshaw, and silenced the 2-pounder. Under intense fire, Private Wakenshaw crawled back to his gun. Although his left arm was blown off, he loaded the gun with one arm and fired five more rounds, setting the tractor on fire and damaging the light gun. A direct hit on the ammunition finally killed him and destroyed the gun. This act of conspicuous gallantry prevented the enemy from using their light gun on the infantry Company which was only 200 yards away. It was through the self sacrifice and courageous devotion to duty of this infantry anti-tank gunner that the Company was enabled to withdraw and to embus in safety." Mike Booker

Casualty records

Records of the Commonwealth War Graves Commission of course also cover the Second World War and can be accessed in the same way as those for the First World War. They provide identical information, although normally details of the next of kin are given. Civilians who lost their lives in air raids or overseas are also included. Details at www.cwgc.org

In the late 1940s the War Office compiled the Army Roll of Honour. It includes much the same information as can be found in the Debt of Honour register, although place of residence and death are also given. It is available online at:

- www.ancestry.co.uk
- www.findmypast.co.uk
- www.military-genealogy.com

Some reference libraries have the Roll on CD.

Medals

Seven medals were issued for each of the major theatres of operations plus service at home. The medal rolls are still with the MOD Medal Office and are unlikely to be transferred to The National Archives for many years yet. However you can still claim your (or your parent's) medals, details at www.veterans.info or write to MOD Medal Office, Building 250, Imjin Barracks, Gloucester GL3 1HW. Former service personnel had to claim their medals as they were not issued automatically. In addition they weren't individually stamped, unlike the ones for the First World War.

An example of the Africa Star awarded for service in North Africa. Author's collection

The citation for the Military Medal awarded to Corporal William Cunningham, Seaforth Highlanders in October 1944. The National Archives WO 373/49

However, details of gallantry awards (such as the Military Medal or the Air Force Cross) are on Documents Online. They include citations which explain in broad details the reasons why the medal was awarded.

Operational records

Provided you know in which unit your father or grandfather (or indeed mother or grandmother) and roughly when, and where, then the operational records can provide a detailed account of their experiences although, unless they were an officer, they are unlikely to be mentioned by name.

War diaries

Again Army battalions kept war diaries, which will give you a detailed day by day account of what the unit got up to. They tend to be rather more detailed than their WW1 equivalents. Of particular interest are the appendices which include daily orders as well as lists of men joining or leaving the unit. The diaries are at The National Archives arranged by theatre of operations in a number of different series

Operation Record Books

These books were compiled on a daily basis by all RAF units. In fact there were two types of ORB: monthly summaries (known as Form 540) and daily summaries (Form 541) which were generally compiled by squadrons. What was recorded inevitably varied, with the most comprehensive accounts generally for squadrons on active service. The records generally become fuller in 1942 and later. Inevitably records for squadrons who flew in the Battle of Britain are sometimes scrappy.

Form 541s include summaries of missions flown, usually with a list of crew members. They were often completed by the squadron intelligence officer after each raid. By going through them day by day you can work out which sorties a man went on.

In addition there may be appendices, which can record men posted in or posted out, and daily orders issued by the commanding officer.

The records are at The National Archives. The most useful series are AIR 27 for squadrons, AIR 28 for other RAF units and AIR 29 for RAF stations and bases.

The Royal Navy

Operation records can be found in three series at The National Archives:

- ADM 199 Case papers relating to all sorts of naval activities from convoys to captains' reports on damage done to individual ships
- ADM 1 Admiralty and Secretariat Papers – arranged by subject (called codes)
- ADM 116 More secret and important papers gathered by the Admiralty. Again arranged by subject codes

In practice there seems to be is no hard and fast rule about which records are to be found where, although it is best to start by going through ADM 199. Fortunately the online catalogue can make checking much simpler than was once the case. Indexes to convoys have recently been added to the catalogue, so you can search by ship's name or convoy number.

Ships' logs aren't helpful as they largely about the weather and navigational positions. In any case many logs are missing.

Submarine logs are in ADM 173. Some logs are humorously annotated with notes and drawings. War patrol reports and associated records, arranged by boat, are in ADM 236, with some records in ADM 199. The Submarine Museum in Gosport may also have information.

Squadron record books for Fleet Air Arm squadrons are in AIR 50. But more information can be found at the FAA Museum at Yeovilton. Also of use is the excellent unofficial Fleet Air Arm Archive at www.fleetairarmarchive.net.

War diaries for Royal Marine units, including the Commandos, are in ADM 202. There is some overlap with war diaries for combined operations in DEFE 2. Again the Royal Marines Museum in Southsea should also be able to help.

Further reading:

Simon Fowler, *Tracing Your Second World War Ancestors* (Countryside Books, 2007)

William Spencer, *Family History in the Wars* (The National Archives, 2007)

Chapter 9

OTHER SOURCES

There are many other resources which can help you find out more about the lives of your ancestors. Unfortunately there's only room to touch on some of the most useful or important ones here, but you might be surprised what you can find online or at archives.

Occupations

Apprentices

Until fairly recently the only way to learn a trade or occupation was to become an apprentice and serve an agreed period where you learnt from a master. For many employers apprentices were little more than cheap labour – which is why legal documents, called indentures, were signed setting out the obligations on both the master and the apprentice. The survival of these indentures is patchy. The Society of Genealogists (SoG) has a reasonable collection and many can also be found at local record offices, particularly in parish and poor law records as male orphans and poor boys in particular were indentured to learn a trade. Livery companies in the City of London also arranged the apprenticeship of many children to trades and these records are generally with the Guildhall Library Manuscripts Department which is part of the London Metropolitan Archives (www.history.ac.uk/gh) or with the company itself. The Goldsmiths' Company has a particularly fine collection.

There is no national index. The nearest that there is are the tax records which were kept between 1710 and 1804, listing names and trades of masters and apprentices and the dates of their indenture. These records are at The National Archives, with copies of the index between 1710 and 1774 at both Kew and the SoG. The records are by no means complete, as there was much evasion and many exemptions were granted.

```
54/23   1760        Wm to Rob Mulley of Diss Norf peruk £10
                PAGEL(L)
52/51   1754  Pagell Jn to Jas Brown of Glasgow comb £8
                PAG(G)ET(T)  PAGIT(T)  PACHIT  PADGET(T)
 7/59   1718  Pagett Abra Wm of Rugby gent to Thos Truesdale of
                                   Stamford Lincs gent £68 5/
 5/16   1716        Ambr Abra of Leicester gent to Jn Manchester
                                        cit & clock £10
13/84   1732  Paget   Chas Jn of Egham Surr to Jos Southam cit & dist £84
22/140  1760  Pagett  Chas to Edw Stevens of St Geo Westr shoe £10
43/118  1714        Dan Joseph of Naveby Leics yeo to Ben Sutton
                     of Loughboro Leics tallch roper & flxd £15
 8/71   1720  Paggett Edw Jn of Mortlake Surr to Letitia Geddings cit
                                        & coop £12 10/
51/274  1752  Padget  Edw to Jas Bennet of Bromsgrove merc £6
48/98   1724  Pagett  Edw Geo decd to Dan Hopkins of Oldswinford Glos
                                            tay £10
15/67   1737  Padget  Geo Geo of Knighton on Team Worcs to Ric Mound
                         of Neen Sollers Salop shoe £5
```

A detail of the eighteenth-century index to apprentices. Society of Genealogists

MERCHANT SEAMEN

Most records relating to merchant seamen are to be found at The National Archives, although if you are interested in the ships your ancestor sailed on the National Maritime Museum is probably the best place to start. Unfortunately records about these seamen are patchy, particularly for the nineteenth century, and can be difficult to use. It helps if you know which ships he served on and whether he was an officer or just an ordinary crew member (and what his specialism was – engineer, radio operator etc). TNA produce a series of readers' signposts and research guides that explain these records in more detail. And a number of series of records have been digitised and are online at www.nationalarchives.gov.uk/documentsonline.

The earliest records date from 1747, when ships' musters and log books first had to be kept and they include lists of crew members. Unfortunately, few early books survive – those that do are in series BT 98. Seamen registered with the Board of Trade between 1835 and 1857 and these records are in various series between BT 112 and BT 120. Indexes of seamen and the ships they served on for the nineteenth century are being prepared by the Crew List Transcription Project at www.crewlist.org.uk/crewlist.html and one or two family history societies – such as Cornwall – have also produced indexes for men from their county.

Details of seamen between 1858 and 1912 are found in the agreements and crew lists for individual ships. The National Archives has a 10 per cent sample. However, the largest collection of these records is with the Maritime History Archive, Memorial University of Newfoundland, St John's, NL A1B 3Y1, Canada www.mun.ca/mha. There are also numerous other short-lived series of records between 1835 and 1913, which may also provide information.

Service records for those who served in the Merchant Navy during the First World War are virtually non-existent. Record cards from the Central Indexed Register, covering the period 1913 to 1920 were destroyed some time ago. All that survives are the cards from a special index for 1918 to 1921. Each card usually gives name, place and date of birth, a short description and a photograph of the man. However you can glean basic information from the Medal Index Cards recording the award of war medals which are available on Documents Online.

If the seaman served after 1942, then the Central Register of Seamen, 1942–1972 may be of use. These records are at THA. Documents Online also has details of campaign medals issued to merchant seamen for service during the Second World War as well as movement cards for individual ships indicating the voyages a ship took.

Lloyd's Captains' Registers can be used for information on masters and mates. They are kept at the Guildhall Library in the City of London, although partial indexes are online at www.history.ac.uk/gh/capintro.htm. More information about researching merchant seamen is at www.mariners-l.co.uk/UK Masters.html. Indeed the whole site is full of valuable information about researching seamen of all ranks.

The *Registers* are also the main source for information on foreign going masters and mates between 1851 and 1947. The registers themselves are kept at Guildhall Library in London, with an incomplete set of microfilm copies at Kew. The Central Indexed Register of Seamen between 1921 and 1941 includes details of all categories of people (men and women) employed at sea, not just ordinary seamen, but also mates, engineers, trimmers, stewards, cooks, etc. The surviving cards are unusual in that they usually include a photograph of the individual together with a date and place of birth, rating, a brief description and a list of ships served on. A name index is also available through TNA's online catalogue. If you are interested the originals are at Southampton City Archives (www.southampton.gov.uk/s-leisure/artsheritage/ history/archives/collections/merhantseamen/centralindex.aspx).

The more recent Central Register of Seamen from 1942 to 1972 comprises docket books and seamen's pouches in series BT 373 and BT 382. The books contain an entry for each seafarer and are arranged alphabetically under several headings. The pouches contain records relating to an individual seaman. An index is also available through TNA's online catalogue.

Further reading:
Chris Watts and Michael Watts, *My Ancestor was a Merchant Seamen* (Society of Genealogists, 2002)
Martin Wilcox, *Fishing and Fishermen* (Pen & Sword, 2008)

The Police

Records of police forces are normally held by either the police themselves or the local record office. The survival of material is patchy, particularly with regard to personnel records of individual officers. The National Archives holds records of London's Metropolitan Police and the Royal Irish Constabulary.

The Metropolitan Police was under the supervision of the Home Secretary, between its foundation in 1829 and the time when responsibility passed to the new Mayor of London in 2000. This is why their records are at Kew.

There are service records between 1829 and 1933, although not everything by any means survives.

The Royal Irish Constabulary was responsible for policing Ireland, with the exception of Dublin, between 1836 and the establishment of the Irish Free State in 1921. The National Archives has service and some pension records for men who served in the force There are plans to put them online.

Further reading:
Stephen Wade, *Tracing Your Police Ancestors* (Pen & Sword, 2009)

The Post Office

The British Postal Museum and Archives has many records of postmen and women going back to the seventeenth century. Find out more at http://postal heritage.org.uk (address in Appendix 4). Records of telephone engineers and other people working on the telecommunications side of the Post Office's work were transferred to British Telecom on the company's creation in 1982

LEAVING THE OFFICES. KILLIGREW STREET EVERY MONDAY AT NOON. AND ARRIVING AT THE CASTLE AND FALCON INN, ALDERSGATE STREET, LONDON, ON THE FOLLOWING SATURDAY. JUNE. 1833.

A post wagon. Author's collection

whose archive can help you research telephone engineers and so on. Again the address is in Appendix 4. Both archives have online catalogues.

Railways

Although the railways were run privately until 1948, their records are largely to be found at The National Archives because they were taken over at nationalisation by British Railways and were eventually passed to Kew.

From the beginning, railway companies employed many hundreds of thousands of men and women. Even the smallest country station had a stationmaster, ticket clerks and porters. At the time of Queen Victoria's Diamond Jubilee, the London and North Western Railway claimed it had 70,000 employees. When the railways were nationalised in 1948, British Railways employed 641,00 people.

Wages were in general low and it was difficult to rise through promotion. It might take twenty years or so to become a train driver. There were compensations, such as sick benefits and pensions. Surprising numbers of women were also employed. Initially women ran station restaurants and bars and laundries, and worked in offices. During the two world wars they were taken on in large numbers to undertake work previously done by men who had joined the forces.

The records are arranged by railway company. You have to have a very good idea which company he (or she) worked for, as well as the type of work they did (signalman, driver, stationmaster etc) as the records are sometimes broken down by occupation. Sometimes if you know the station or depot where he was based that can often help identify the company who employed him.

The survival of records is patchy and each company kept records in their own way so there is little standardisation. They are most complete for the Great Western Railway (GWR or God's Wonderful Railway to enthusiasts!) and little may survive for the many small companies of the mid-Victorian period. The sort of records you are likely to come across are:

- Staff registers
- Pay records and registers
- Minutes often include notes about the appointment, promotion and dismissal of staff
- Pension and benefits records
- Accidents – all serious accidents were investigated in great detail
- Staff magazines contain a lot about the movement of staff and their retirement, as well as other stories such as the award of a medal for a prize-winning allotment

At the time of writing very little has been digitised and placed online although an index to men who served with the North London Railway is in TNA's online catalogue. However, staff records for the larger railway companies are being digitalised and these should be online during 2011.

An interesting website with many extracts from records including accident investigation reports is www.railwaysarchive.co.uk.

Local archives may well have records about railways in their areas. Cheshire Record Office for example has an index and other records about the men who worked at the Crewe Works. Newspapers are also another useful source as they will describe fatal accidents and the retirements of prominent local officials. Records held by the National Railway Museum in York, however, are very largely about the technical side of railways.

GREAT EASTERN RAILWAY MAGAZINE.

191

STAFF NOTES.

Liverpool Street.—On Saturday, May 15th, in the Office of 124 Hamilton House, Liverpool Street, Mr. Percy Syder was presented with an illuminated address from the whole of the members of his late staff, on the occasion of his appointment to Ipswich.

The chair was taken by Mr. A. Barker, who, after a few appropriately worded remarks, called upon Mr. T. G. A. Miles to make the presentation. The latter spoke of the spontaneous and unanimous desire of all the staff until recently serving under the directions of Mr. Syder at Liverpool Street (with whom he associated absentees nobly engaged in their country's cause), to show in some tangible form the esteem in which Mr. Syder was held, amplifying his remarks in expressions of mixed feelings of regret and pleasure : regret in losing one who had always extended to them a ready sympathy and kindly consideration, and pleasure in the knowledge that he had been selected for the

important position of District Goods Manager at Ipswich. Mr. Miles concluded with very hearty wishes for his future prosperity, and an enjoyment of good health.

Mr. Syder, in accepting the address, thanked all for their kind expressions, adding that if anything tangible were necessary to remind him of the willing assistance afforded him at all times by each member of his late staff, and the very pleasant social excursions they had had together, it could not have taken a more appreciable form than that of which he was the proud recipient. He also paid a very high tribute to those absent ones engaged in the defence of the country against a ruthless enemy, hoping, in which hope he knew he was but re-echoing what was in the minds of all present, that they would come through the ordeal "safe and sound."

Norwich. — On the 22nd March, Mr. H. W. C. Drury, the District Locomotive Superintendent, on behalf of the departmental foremen and clerical staff, presented to Mr. W. Mann, one of his clerks,

MR. AND MRS. MANN.

a handsome marble clock on the occasion of his marriage, with the best wishes of all for future happiness.

◆ ◆ ◆

Bishopsgate. — INSPECTOR W. BOLTON, who succeeds Mr. Archer as inspector at Bishopsgate Goods Station, was presented with a marble clock and ornaments on the occasion of his promotion. Mr. Bolton joined the service in August, 1888.

MR. W. BOLTON.　　　MR. F. TURNER.

A presentation of a marble clock was also made to Foreman F. Turner on his transfer to Cambridge Heath stables, as a mark of the respect in which he was held, Mr. Turner entered the service in June, 1889.

◆ ◆ ◆

March.—On Easter Monday the marriage of Mr. Percy W. Millington, travelling ticket collector, Norwich, took place at St. John's Church, March. As a token of their good wishes, the travelling ticket

MR. AND MRS. MILLINGTON.

collectors and the Norwich dining car staff presented him with a coal vase and a pair of ornaments.

A page from the Great Eastern Railway staff magazine with stories about the marriage and retirement of colleagues. Author's collection

Further reading:
Di Drummond, *Tracing Your Railway Ancestors* (Pen & Sword, 2010)
Cliff Edwards, *Railway Records: A Guide to Sources* (Public Record Office, 2001)
The Railway Ancestors FHS (www.railwayancestors.org.uk) has lots of resources to help you research railway staff

Immigration and Emigration

There are surprisingly few records about people who settled in Britain or left these shores to make new lives for themselves abroad.

During the nineteenth century Britain prided itself on the liberal attitude it had towards groups of foreigners in the country – restrictions were first only introduced a hundred or so years ago to try to control Jewish migration from Russia and Poland. Unlike most other European countries aliens did not have to register with the police until 1914, so a potentially a major source of records does not exist.

Similarly the government was always keen to encourage emigration, particularly of the poor to British colonies, but was less enthusiastic about paying for their removal. The millions of Irish men and women who found their way to America in the wake of the Great Famine in the 1840s, did so largely under their own steam. The major exception to this was the transportation of thousands of petty criminals to Australia in the first half of the nineteenth century.

Hundreds of thousands of people from across the British Isles left for new and generally better lives overseas before the Second World War paying their way as they did. However about a third eventually returned, either because things did not work out as they hoped, because they prospered or because of homesickness. This should be remembered when looking for ancestors who disappeared either for good or for a period of time.

Immigration

It may be clear that you already have immigrants in your family tree, or it may be something you discover as you go about your research. Many people, for example, find that they have Huguenot ancestors, that is the French Protestant refugees who settled in Britain about 1700. Fortunately a lot of research has been done into these people which has been published by the Huguenot Society. Many of these publications can be consulted at the Society of Genealogists.

Most migrants to Britain were attracted by economic opportunities, perhaps as waiters or governesses, or just drifted here for one reason or another. The great writer Joseph Conrad, for example, arrived as a penniless Polish sailor. By the end of the nineteenth century many large towns and cities had small close-knit communities of Polish or Russian Jews, Italians and Germans – although the Germans were large expelled during and after the First World War. Only the East End of London and the docks areas elsewhere (especially Liverpool, Cardiff and Glasgow) had anything approaching the melting-pot of nationalities common in America. By far the largest community, however, was the Irish – but as they were regarded as British citizens there are no records of their departure from Ireland and very few which specifically identify them as such in Britain.

Foreigners should appear on the census – great efforts were made by the authorities to ensure that they completed the forms, although normally only the country of their birth (and not the town or province) is included.

Passenger lists begin in 1878, but were only kept for ships who arrived in Britain from outside Europe and the Mediterranean. They are available online fully indexed at ancestory.co.uk. However there are several earlier series of records that might help, including certificates of aliens arriving in UK between 1836 and 1852, arranged by port of arrival. Each certificate gives the individual's nationality, their profession, date of arrival, last country visited and signature. In addition there are incomplete lists of immigrants arriving from Europe between 1836 and 1869, drawn up by master of ship on which they arrived. These lists and other nineteenth century immigration records are also available at www.ancestry.co.uk.

Few people became naturalised, except by marriage, because it was an expensive process and conferred few additional rights. Before 1844 to become a naturalised citizen required an act of parliament. Most people chose the cheaper option of denization which was to become a British subject without the full rights of a citizen, that is they could not hold public office or inherit land. There are records of denization and naturalisation from the fifteenth century onwards. Between 1844 and 1986 these records can be found in Home Office records. Some indexes are available online. Announcements (and indexes) for both naturalisation and denization were also published in *London Gazette*. The *Gazette* is online at www.london-gazette.co.uk, although the indexing could be better.

Two family history societies may be able to help if you are descended from Germans or Italians: http://www.agfhs.org.uk and www.anglo-italianfhs. org.uk respectively.

P.M. 23.

Name of Ship "PARTHIA" Port of Arrival LIVERPOOL Date of Arrival 28th MARCH 19 53
Steamship Line THE CUNARD STEAM-SHIP COMPANY LIMITED. Whence Arrived NEW YORK
CUNARD WHITE STAR.

NAMES AND DESCRIPTIONS OF BRITISH PASSENGERS

28 MAR 1953 LIVERPOOL

Port of Embarkation	Port at which Passengers have been landed	NAMES OF PASSENGERS		CLASS	Age	Proposed Address in the United Kingdom	Profession, Occupation or Calling of Passengers	Country of Last Permanent Residence	Country of Intended Future Permanent Residence
N.Y. 21	Liverpool	COOKE	Dorothy	First	27	Ashfield House, Aspull, Nr. Wigan.	Student	England	England 1
" 22	"	DAVIDSON	John	"	32	Woodland Hotel, Bernhill, Dundee.	Accountant	Venezuela	Foreign 1
" 23	"	DAVIDSON	Joan	"	32	As above	Housewife	Venezuela	Foreign 1
" 24	"	DAVIDSON	David	"	5	As above	Child	Venezuela	Foreign 1
" 25	"	DAVIS	Richard	"	55	Smethwick, Staffs., 5, St. Albans Rd.,	Construction Engineer	England	England 1
" 26	"	FANE	Harry	"	37	10, Park Lane, Great Harwood, Lancs.	Govt. Official	U.S.A.	Foreign 1
" 27	"	FANE	Stella	"	37	As above	Housewife	U.S.A.	Foreign 1
" 28	"	FANE	Kathleen	"	4	As above	Child	U.S.A.	Foreign 1
" 29	"	FRASER	John	"	41	c/oGray, 34 Nth. Wellington St., Dundee, Scotland.	Engineer	Columbia, S.A.	1
" 30	"	FRASER	Ann	"	7	As above	Student	Columbia S.A.	1
" 31	"	FRASER	Angus	"	1	As above	Child	Columbia S.A.	1
" 32	"	FRASER	Williamina	"	41	As above	Housewife	Columbia S.A.	1
" 33	"	FYFE	Margaret	"	43	10, Auchendoon, Cres. Ayr, Scotland.	None	Scotland	Scotland 1
" 34	"	FYFE	Fiona	"	16	As above	Student	Scotland	Scotland 1
" 35	"	GAFFNEY	Helen	"	59	c/o 39. Thrusheraig Rd. Paisly, Scotland.	Housewife	U.S.A.	1
" 36	"	HALE	Elizabeth	"	25	Longcroft, Aldeburgh, Suffolk.	Horticultural Research	England	England 1
" 37	"	HOWARD	Edward	"	47	Lingcroft, Grangecourt Rd., Harpenden, Herts.	Engineer	England	England 1
" 38	"	HOWARD	Mary	"	39	As above	Housewife	England	England 1
" 39	"	JAGO	John	"	45	Old Lodge, Fitchfield, Hants.	Royal Navy	U.S.A.	1
" 40	"	JAGO	June	"	41	As above	Housewife	U.S.A.	1
" 41	"	JAGO	John	"	3	As above	Child	U.S.A.	1
" 42	"	JAGO	Suzanne	"	2	As above	Child	U.S.A.	1
" 43	"	JONAS	Jack	"	24	3, Alma Rd., Carshalton Surrey.	Marine Engineer	England	England 1
" 44	"	KIRKPATRICK	Winifred	"	47	"Moverton",Stanford-Bridge, Worcestershire.	None	Canada	1
" 45	"	LIMOND	Eric	"	39	7, Belgrave Drive, Pooltown Rd., Whitby, Wirral, Cheshire.	Staff Dept., Oil Co.	Venezuela S.A.	1
" 46	"	LIMOND	Elsie	"	38	As above	Housewife	Venezuela S.A.	1
" 47	"	LIMOND	Mary	"	77	As above	None	Venezuela S.A.	1
" 48	"	LIMOND	Eric	"	5	As above	Child	Venezuela S.A.	1
" 49	"	LISTER	Charles	"	57	Hotel Park Lane, Piccadilly, London W.1.	Banana Broker	Victoria B.C. Canada	1
" 50	"	LISTER	Margaret	"	45	As above	Housewife	Canada	1
" 51	"	LYONS	Joel	"	66	239, Woolton Rd., Liverpool, 16.	Cafe Prop.	England	England 1
" 52	"	MACDONALD	Donald	"	70	1, Croft Rd., Tarbert, Argyll.	Headmaster(Ret)	Scotland	Scotland 1
" 53	"	MACDONALD	Agnes	"	69	As above	Housewife	Scotland	Scotland 1

The inward bound passenger list for SS Parthia for March 1953 with the entry for my wife's grandfather Joel Lyons. TWA DT26/1296/81 (Ancestry)

A passenger list for the SS Hesperian which left Glasgow for Quebec and Montreal in June 1909. TNA BT 27 1206 (Findmypast)

Emigration

Frankly the best place to start is with the country where they emigrated to – normally the United States or colonies within the Empire – as their records are likely to be much fuller. For example passenger lists for ships arriving in the United States begin in 1819, their British equivalents for ships leaving our shores don't start until 1890. And there are detailed records for arrivals in Sydney from 1854. There are many books and websites to help hunt down ancestors who sought a new life across the Atlantic or in Australasia much easier.

Passenger lists begin in 1890 for ships whose destinations were outside Europe and the Mediterranean and finish in 1960. They list everybody in the party, their ages and occupations as well as their address in Britain and are online at www.findmypast.co.uk.

There were very few government schemes to encourage emigration, although some records do exist. Perhaps the best known of these was the doomed plan by the New Zealand Company to recreate an idealised British society in the untamed New Zealand bush – there are detailed records of the applicants, together with reference and other notes. Another scheme was to encourage soldiers to settle in the colonies on their discharge as the basis of a militia should trouble arise with the natives. Records for both schemes are at The National Archives although neither are online.

The British in India

The British have a long association with the Indian sub-continent. The first Brits arrived as traders four centuries ago. By the mid-eighteenth century the Honourable East India Company (HEIC or EIC) had become the dominant power. After the Indian Mutiny of 1757 the Company was replaced by a new Government of India. Many young men went to India to seek their fortunes working for the Company and its successor in a variety of posts from railway driver to district officer. In particular many joined the Bengal, Madras or Bombay armies which were absorbed into the Indian Army. However, the British Army also had barracks and stationed men here. As a result it is easy confuse the two – the assumption being that a British soldier serving in India was with the British Army. This is the case if you are researching an ordinary soldier or non-commissioned officer of European stock who served in the Sub-Continent after 1857. However, officers could have been in either Army.

It is easy to tell either from the name of the regiment he served with or by checking in the printed Army Lists.

Surviving records of the East India Company and the Government of India are largely with the British Library, Asia, Pacific & Africa Collections, 96 Euston Road, London NW1 2DB, www.bl.uk/catalogues/iofhs.shtml. There are various databases on the website which may be of use.

Further reading:
Roger Kershaw, *Migration Records* (The National Archives Publications, 2009)
Ian Baxter, *Baxter's guide: Biographical sources in the India Office Records* (FIBIS, 2007)
Rosemary Wenzerul, *Tracing Your Jewish Ancestors* (Pen & Sword, 2008)

The Family in British India Society (FIBIS) maintains an excellent website and wiki at www.fibis.org.

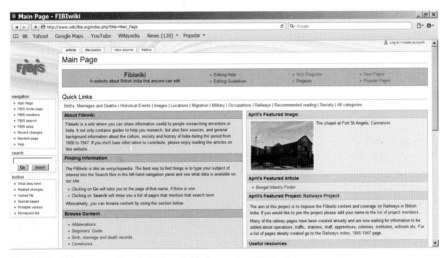

The FIBIwiki can provide a lot of useful information. FIBIwiki

Miscellaneous

Changes of name

There is no legal obligation to register a change of name – provided you do not attempt to deceive others you can call yourself what you like. Indeed one of the pitfalls of family history research are ancestors who were always known by nicknames or did not use their given names, which may be at variance with how they are referred to in birth, marriage or death certificates.

However, people have always wanted to formally change their name – a common reason in the nineteenth century was in accordance with the terms of a will in order to inherit an estate. During the First World War many German emigrants adopted British surnames in order to avoid persecution. The National Archives has indexes of these changes, often known as deed polls, from 1851. In addition notices about the intention to change names have been advertised in the *London Gazette* (the government's official newspaper) since 1914 – online at www.london-gazette.co.uk.

Criminals

Introduction

It has always been a primary duty of the state to protect the citizen from wrongdoers and to provide justice to those who required it. This has meant that a great many records relating to the criminal system have been created over the centuries.

If you are interested in tracing the criminal career of an ancestor, it is important to know, or be able to hazard a guess about, the following:

- where and when he or she was convicted, and
- what the offence was

For the nineteenth and early part of the twentieth century there are reasonable registers of criminals or prisoners, and it is much easier to work back to the court records from these registers than to go straight to the court records themselves.

Records created by the courts are notoriously difficult to use. They are often little more than notes about the progress of a case through the courts, rather than a verbatim account of the trial. Even the verdict may be difficult to find. To add to the difficulties, before 1733 legal records were in Latin, and the records themselves can be very hard to read.

Location of records
Records are split between The National Archives and local record offices. It is not always clear what is held where.

In general, TNA holds records of:

- Central courts, for both criminal and civil matters (such as assizes, high courts, chancery, exchequer, court of common pleas)
- Central Criminal Court for London (the Old Bailey) from 1834. A detailed website for trials at the Old Bailey between 1674 and 1913 is at www.oldbaileyonline.org.
- The Metropolitan Police from 1829
- Criminal registers, 1791–1892. Initially for Middlesex and later for the whole country. These are online at www.ancestry.co.uk
- Registers or calendars of prisoners, 1770–1913, covering the whole country including prison hulks. There are also other records for prisons in Middlesex. Some records are also online at Ancestry
- Bankrupts and debtors

Local record offices may hold records of:

- Petty sessions (that is magistrates or police courts), quarter sessions to 1972 (local criminal courts), and Crown Courts from 1972
- Quarter Sessions – detailed indexes to these records are at www.national archives.gov.uk/a2a
- County courts (local civil courts)
- The constabulary for that county
- Calendars (registers) of prisoners in that county

Other sources, which might be of use, include:

- Newspapers – which often had detailed accounts of important trials, and listed prisoners sent down by magistrates (see Chapter 10)
- Some, mainly sixteenth and seventeenth century, quarter session and assize records have been published by local record societies. Both the Society of Genealogists and TNA libraries have an almost complete set of these publications

Further reading:

Michelle Cale, *Law and Society: An Introduction to Sources for Criminal and Legal History from 1800* (Public Record Office,1996)

David T Hawkings, *Criminal ancestors, a guide to historical criminal records in England and Wales* (2nd edition, The History Press, 2009)

Ruth Paley & Simon Fowler, *Family Skeletons* (TNA, 2006)

Stephen Wade, *Tracing your Criminal Ancestors* (Pen & Sword, 2009)

Ancestry also has some records of unfortunates transported to Australia, but the best source (and it's free) is Convict Transportation Register (1787–1867) at www.slq.qld.gov.au/info/fh/convicts which has names of convicts, details of their crimes and the ships they were transported in.

Freemasons

Freemasonry have long had a reputation for secrecy, but in fact if your ancestor was "on the square" (and he may well have been if was a policeman or worked in local government) there are actually lots of records which will tell you about his membership and help identify any regalia (known as "jewels") that you may have inherited. The Freemasons' Library and Museum at Freemasons' Hall, 60 Great Queen Street, London WC2B 5AZ.

www.freemasonry.london.museum maintain detailed records from the eighteenth century onwards. The website also has a number of useful databases and links to lists of freemasons. In addition local lodges had to supply annual lists of members to Quarter Sessions. These lists, where they survive, should be in papers of the Sessions at local record offices.

Freemasons' regalia can easily be confused with that worn by members of friendly societies. Millions of people once belonged to these societies as a way of receiving benefits in time of unemployment or sickness. There were hundreds of different societies, most of which have long disappeared. If you know which society you ancestor belonged to then searching the National Register of Archives (www.nationalarchives.gov.uk/nra) may turn up where the records are now kept.

POOR LAW AND CHARITY RECORDS

Until the introduction of the welfare state the poor (particularly orphans, the sick and the elderly) received support under a system known as the Poor Law. Before 1834 it was administered by individual towns and parishes. The system was radically overhauled in 1834, and between then and 1929 it was run by a system of 650 Poor Law Unions administered by Boards of Guardians which ran the local workhouse and paid small allowances ("out-relief") where appropriate. The new system was cordially disliked by the poor because of the harsh conditions and petty regulations it imposed.

Was my ancestor a pauper?
You may be able to identify whether an ancestor was a pauper in the following ways:

- family memories or records
- identified as such in birth, death or marriage certificates.
- whether they are listed in the census as being in the workhouse, as a 'pauper', or in receipt of 'parochial relief'
- individuals, especially widows, who were very old and from a poor background
- mothers of illegitimate children

Because the Poor Law was largely administered locally records are likely to be at local record offices. You might come across types of documents such as these:

Old Poor Law before 1834
- Overseers' accounts list who received help and the type of help offered
- Poor rate books recording who paid the poor rate. These records continue after 1834
- Settlement and bastardy records which describe attempts to return paupers to their place of origin and find the fathers of illegitimate children
- Vestry minute books, and records of boroughs, often include material about the administration of the poor law locally

New poor law after 1834
Amongst the most important series of records are:

- Admission and discharge registers to the workhouse. They record the names and ages of everybody admitted and discharged, with the reason for discharge
- Creed registers, giving religion of each applicant together with other personal details
- Minute books of Boards of Guardians, together with committee books, record almost every decision made about the running of the Union. The

fate of individual paupers is often described. Detailed accounts of Guardians' meetings usually appear in local newspapers

- Outdoor relief order books recording applicant, amount and the period the relief was to be paid for
- Published lists of accounts and indoor and outdoor paupers relieved. They may give other information, such as lists of pauper children sent to Canada
- Registers of births, baptisms, burials and deaths in the workhouse

Further reading:
Robert Burlison, *Tracing Your Pauper Ancestors* (Pen & Sword, 2008)
Simon Fowler, *Poor Law Records – how to make the best use of them* (Family History Partnership, 2011)
Jeremy Gibson, *Poor Law Union Records* (Family History Partnership, 2007)

Records are almost all at local record offices. Relatively little is yet online. An increasing proportion of poor law records for London are available at www.ancestry.co.uk/London. An excellent website devoted to workhouses and the experiences of people in them is www.workhouses.org.uk.

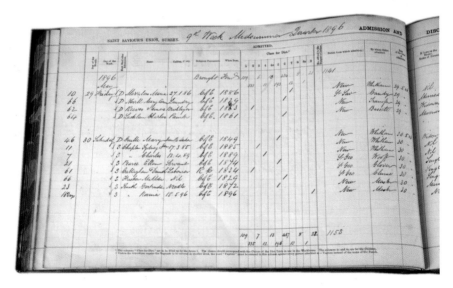

A page from the Admission Register of the Lambeth Workhouse showing the entry for Charles Chaplin and his brother. Ancestry.co.uk/London Metropolitan Archives

SCHOOL RECORDS

Introduction

Education was just as important for our ancestors as it is for ourselves. Even in medieval times most children had a year or two of schooling, although few needed to be able to read or write. It was only late in the nineteenth century that education became compulsory: much later than in Scotland or our major industrial competitors. Indeed some historians have argued that Britain's economic decline has been largely due to poor schooling and training.

Before the introduction of state run schools in 1870 schools came in three basic types, although there was some overlap between the three:

- Public schools, such as Eton, Harrow and Winchester, where the upper classes tended to educate their sons in the classics with only a modicum of science and other useful topics. *Tom Brown's Schooldays* is of course a classic description of Rugby School in mid-Victorian times
- Denominational schools organised by a local church or national religious charity. During the nineteenth century a network of "National" (Church of England) and "British" (non-conformist) schools grew up around the country. They often formed the backbone of later local authority primary schools
- Lesser schools which might vary from dame schools where a widow might eke out a meagre pension teaching the ABC to village children to boarding schools for orphans, workhouse children or the unwanted. Dotheboys Hall presided over by Wackford Squeers, immortalised the type in *Nicholas Nickleby*

State involvement in education came late, largely because of inter-denominational rivalry. The 1870 Education Act set up local education boards to establish and run schools where none existed. Schooling for children between six and ten was not made compulsory until 1880. School leaving age has been subsequently raised thus:

- 11: 1893
- 12: 1899
- 14: 1918
- 15: 1947
- 16: 1965
- 18: 2013 (proposed)

Until after the Second World War it was comparatively rare for children, especially those from poorer backgrounds, to receive secondary education, often because it depended on the award of a grant from the local authority. Girls in particular were discriminated against. Very few people, men or women, went onto university until the 1960s. Naturally, the position was somewhat different for the upper classes who could afford to send their children to both public schools and university.

The 1944 Education Act in effect established universal secondary education for everybody. The 1960s saw an expansion of tertiary education, that is universities, polytechnics and the Open University.

The records
Most local authority school records are held by the local or county record office. Public schools have their own archives. Records for individual schools are a bit patchy and more recent ones may not be available. The records which are likely to be of most use are:

- Attendance registers: name the child and give the date of admission, father's name and address (and sometimes the mother), date of birth, the name of previous schools, and date of leaving. Some registers also record when a child left school and the destination. Registers start from the 1870s
- School logbooks: completed by the school head on a daily basis. Individual pupils are likely to be mentioned if they were either disciplined or away sick. They start in the 1840s
- The National Archives holds records of inspections of schools which can be very interesting. Individual pupils are rarely mentioned, although their teachers often are
- The schools themselves may have some records such as school magazines, and old boys or girls association magazines

Some records of public schools may have been deposited with local record offices, but many have retained their own archives. Many public schools have published lists of former pupils. The largest collections of these are at the Society of Genealogists.

The older universities, too, have published lists of graduates, often with a reasonable amount of additional biographical material. Again, the SoG has a large collection. University and college archives may well also have other material on former students and the lives that they led.

Teachers

There have of course always been teachers, but it took until the end of the nineteenth century for teaching to become a profession with the growth of proper training colleges. Before then teachers learnt on the job. The early nineteenth century saw the development of the monitorial system, older children in their teens who were supposed to instruct the younger ones in their lessons. The monitors themselves were taught by the teachers.

Prior to the early nineteenth century few documents mention teachers. Appointments and dismissals may sometimes be found in surviving school records themselves, in parish records, or educational charity records. From the mid-nineteenth century teacher training was largely carried out by the denominations.

Records of some Anglican teachers are held by the Church of England Record Centre (www.cofe.anglican.org/about/librariesandarchives/recordscentre/). Many records of non-conformist teaches are with the British and Foreign School Society (www.bfss.org.uk/archive.shtml). Other records may be at teacher training colleges themselves or deposited at local record offices.

Chapter 10

PRINTED SOURCES

You may not always need to spend hours trying to read bad handwriting, there are lots of printed sources that might well contain the names of ancestors and they are much easier to use. Generally they are to be found at local libraries and record offices, although an increasing proportion is to be found online. If you want to see the sort of thing that might be available check out The Original Record's website www.theoriginalrecord.com.

Directories

Directories are published lists of names, usually arranged by address or by trade or profession. The first directories appeared in the mid-eighteenth century, but they really came into their own in the 1840s and 1850s. The largest publisher of directories was set up by Francis Kelley in 1845. Originally they were lists of local gentry and traders, but by the end of the nineteenth century there were several different types:

- Street directories – listing by street and house by house the householder, sometimes with their occupation;
- Trade directories – list of local tradesmen, small businesses and the like, with addresses
- Court directories – listing the 'more respectable' middle and upper class members of the local community

In addition many professions produce directories of practitioners. The most famous of these is *Crockford's Clerical Directory*, which has been published since 1858 listing priests in the Church of England. Other famous directories are the *Law List* and the *Medical List* for barristers and doctors respectively. Directories will often include short biographies of members or list promotions and honours awarded. The Society of Genealogists has a large collection. Otherwise libraries and archives maintained by professional societies and associations usually have complete sets and may be willing to check them for you (as well as provide additional information from their records).

A page from the 1900 trade and street directory for Kew. Author's collection

Incidentally if you are researching an Anglican clergyman between about 1550 and 1850 it is worth checking out the Clergy Database at www.theclergy database.org.uk.

There is no national collection of street or trade directories, although both Guildhall Library in the City of London and the Society of Genealogists have large collections. Local studies libraries usually have directories for their area. Many directories are now available on CD. The largest producer is S&N Genealogical Publications at www.sandn.net.

However, the best place to start is with the free Historical Directories website, which has digitised a large number from the late nineteenth and early twentieth century – www.historicaldirectories.org.

You can use directories for:

- Checking the address of people, although you should remember that the information in directories was often a year or two out of date at the time of publication. If a family was not where they should have been on census night, it is worth checking to see whether they have moved around the corner
- Checking occupations. In working class families the householder may have continually have been changing jobs, so the entry in the directory may be different to that which appears on the census
- Trace the career of a professional person through the professional directories

Rather less useful are telephone directories partly because they only give name and address, but more importantly it was not until the 1960s that most households had a telephone so they are not very complete. But occasionally they can be useful. I remember using them to find the home address of Britain's greatest gangster between the wars in respectable Hove. From 1880 to the mid-1980s they are available online at Ancestry.co.uk.

Electoral registers

Electoral registers begin in 1832. They show people entitled to vote, house by house, arranged in street and polling district order. The franchise remained fairly restricted until 1918, when all men over 21 and women over 30 gained the right to vote. Women over 21 could vote from 1928. For this reason they are of limited use. Until 1948 the type of franchise under which the elector was entitled to vote is also shown, and this may give a clue to an ancestor's wealth. Occasionally lists of men and women entitled to serve on juries may also be included.

Electoral registers are normally kept by local libraries, although the British Library has a complete set from 1947 and a patchy collection from 1832. The best introduction is Jeremy Gibson, *Electoral Registers 1832–1948* (4th edition, Family History Partnership, 2008). Registers for Birmingham are available at www.midlandshistoricaldata.org for a fee, but few other registers are yet online. A guide to the British Library's holdings is at www.bl.uk/reshelp/findhelprestype/offpubs/electreg/electoral.html.

POLLING DISTRICT K.				PARISH OF TWICKENHAM
(1)	(2)		(3)	(4)
No.	Franchise. (a) Parlia- (b) Local mentary. Govt.		Names in full. Surname first.	Residence or Property and abode of non-resident
1	R	O	Crame, George Amos	1 AMYAND COTTAGES
2	NM	—	aCrame, George William	1
3	HO	HO	Crame, Selina Charlotte	1
4	R	O	Hewett, Frederick	2
5	R	—	Hewett, Joseph	2
6	HO	HO	Hewett, Louisa Maud	2
7	HO	HO	Lambourne, Alice Maud	3
8	R	O	Lambourne, Richard	3
9	R	—	Lambourne, Richard Edward	3
10	R	—	Van Niekerk, Daniel	3
11	O	O	Brand, Alice	4
12	O	O	Harrington, Elizabeth	4
13	HO	HO	Brown, Fanny	5
14	R	—	Brown, Frank	5
15	R	O	Brown, Frederick	5
16	HO	HO	White, Annie	6
17	R	O	White, Eanes Frederick	6
18	R	O	Hart, Herbert Joe	7
19	O	O	Parratt, Jane	7
20	R	O	Samuels, Ernest Fred	8
21	HO	HO	Samuels, Kate	8
22	HO	HO	Sharp, Laura Mabel	9
23	R	O	Sharp, Reginald John	9
24	R	O	Davis, Joseph James	10
25	HO	HO	Davis, Mabel Alice	10
26	HC	HO	Messom, Ada Frances	1 AMYAND PARK GARDENS
27	R	O	Messom, Francis William —8 J	1
28	R	O	Crampton, Charles Stanhope—J	3
29	HO	HO	Crampton, Muriel	3

A electoral register from the 1920s for Twickenham. London Borough of Richmond upon Thames

Before 1872 how electors voted were recorded in Poll Books. A list of surviving poll books are given in Jeremy Gibson and Colin Rogers, *Poll Books c1696–1872: a Directory to holdings in Great Britain* (4th edition, Family History Partnership, 2008). A few poll books have been published on CD by S&N Genealogical Supplies.

Newspapers

Newspapers are an important if under used resource for family history, largely because they are thought to be difficult to use. They include stories about disasters, court proceedings, campaigns, major events and the people

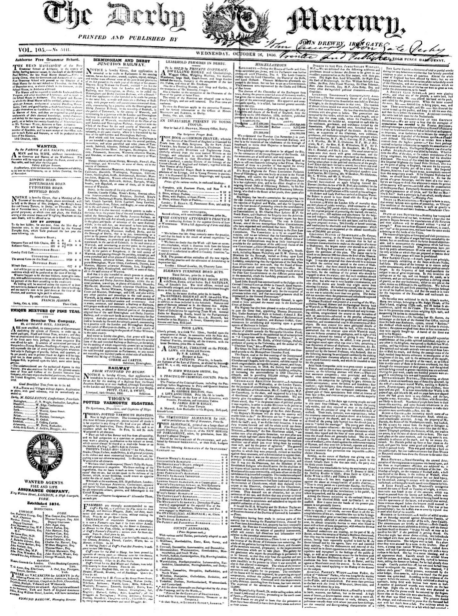

The front page of the Derby Mercury *for 6 March 1835 showing the range of advertisements.*
British Library

NINETEENTH-CENTURY NEWSPAPERS

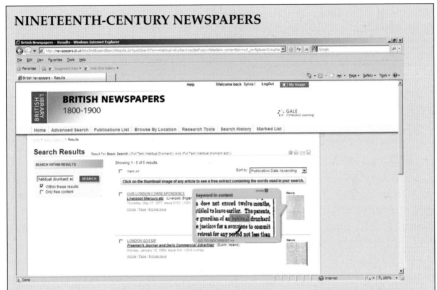

The search page for the British Library's Nineteenth Century Newspaper website. British Library

The British Library has placed online, at http://newspapers.bl.uk/blcs, digitised editions of fifty newspapers and magazines published between 1800 and 1899, including many local papers. It is just a sample at present, but more are likely to be added over the next few years.

This is a major new resource for family historians. Realistically for the first time it is possible to use these newspapers to complement other records and so build up a rounder portrait of our forebears, with information that would not be possible to obtain elsewhere.

Stories about four of my ancestors, all called Paul Belcher, appear in half a dozen different newspapers here. Only once could it be said that they stepped into the limelight. In May 1854, as Revd Paul Belcher was announcing the banns for an unfortunately unnamed couple at Heather parish church in Leicestershire the father of the bride objected: "I forbid the banns in this church and everywhere else becos hers too young and hers robbed me." This was picked up first by the *Derby Mercury* and then by other papers across the country.

If you are lucky your local library subscribes so you will be able to use it at home for free. Otherwise you have to pay for access. At the time of writing it costs £6.99 for a day's access or £9.99 for seven days. It's easy to search by name or place. You can do a preliminary search for free which will produce short extracts containing just enough information to confirm whether the story is about your ancestor or not.

caught up in them, for at least three centuries. The doings of everyone from politicians to pastry cooks have been grist to the reporter's mill. Then there are the advertisements, not to mention government notices, and the columns filled with births, deaths and marriages – all the grind of daily local and national life.

You never know what you're going to find, which is why they are a joy and a curse to use. It is very easy to be sidetracked by the advertisements for patent medicines, and odd news stories. Indeed the biggest problem is the vast amount of information you may have to sift through before you get to the item you are looking for.

The first newspapers were published in the seventeenth century. Their news content however was often taken from other papers, although there are lots of stories about unusual phenomena. The newspaper, as we know it today, is really a product of the nineteenth century. The telegraph and better posts meant that news stories would be up-to-date. Better printing presses meant more and cheaper newspapers. By 1900 the first picture newspapers, including the *Daily Mail* and *Daily Mirror*, were published with a mass audience in mind. The mid-nineteenth century also saw the rise of the "local rag" and most towns soon had two or three rival papers.

Stories tend to fall into three categories: those which confirm information found elsewhere and those which provide leads to be followed up in other sources; but most offer new insights into their lives from burglaries to attendance at weddings. So newspapers could be used for the following:

- To find published notices of births, marriages and deaths
- Coverage of marriages and funerals – this may tell you who were present and what the ceremony was like. There may also be obituaries of prominent local people
- Sports events, school speech days, annual dinners, and, especially, court cases were all likely to receive coverage and include names of prize-winners or witnesses
- Unusual deaths – accidents or deaths in suspicious circumstances were likely to be described often in depth. There are likely to be verbatim accounts of proceedings of coroners' courts and extensive coverage of a murder investigations

During the two world wars there may be letters from local men describing life in the services, short obituaries of the deceased and photographs.

Advertisements for local businesses and the sale of land can also be interesting if your ancestor was a butcher or bought a pub.

Local newspapers are generally to be found at record offices or at central libraries. They are almost always produced on microfilm which can be quite tiring to use. Rarely are they indexed to any great degree, so you will need to know roughly when the event you are interested took place. On the other hand many local studies libraries maintain large and well-indexed collections of press cuttings which are generally easier to use.

A national collection of newspapers is at the British Newspaper Library. This outpost of the British Library at Colindale in north London holds over 50,000 different titles of newspapers, magazines and journals from across the United Kingdom and indeed across the world dating back to the end of the seventeenth century. Its catalogue is online at http://catalogue.bl.uk. Colindale will be closing by 2012 and the collection is moving to the main British Library building in central London. As a result an increasing

---

NATIONAL NEWSPAPERS ONLINE

The full searchable archives of three great national papers are now available online for a fee:

The [Manchester] *Guardian* (and *Observer*) http://archive.guardian.co.uk
The Scotsman http://archive.scotsman.com
The Times (and *Sunday Times*) http://archive.timesonline.co.uk. Local libraries may have an older version of The Times Digital Archive which you may be able to access at home.

You might think that your ancestors would never appear in a national newspaper, but until well after the Second World War they included lots of local stories, such as announcements of births, marriages and deaths or court appearances. So if your people came from Manchester and the North West it is well worth checking *The Guardian*, for London and the Home Counties, *The Times*, and in Edinburgh and Lothian *The Scotsman*. The indexes are easy to use and are free. You only pay to download individual stories.

proportion of papers, certainly for the nineteenth century, are being digitised and can be found at http://newspapers.bl.uk (see box).

If your ancestor worked in a particular trade or profession especially if they reached a position of prominence or spent their whole career with a particular company, then it might be worth looking out for trade journals and company magazines. By the end of the nineteenth century most industries supported a journal providing news, gossip and details of the latest developments. Large factories or companies also published similar monthly magazines for staff, as did hospitals and schools for staff, patients or pupils, and their families and friends. The largest collection is at the British Newspaper Library, but The National Archives has many railway staff magazines and local libraries may also have copies of magazines and journals for local industries.

Richmond-upon-Thames Local Studies Library, for example, has copies of the magazine produced by patients at the Royal Star and Garter Home on

A page from the London Gazette *showing obituaries "and natural occurences".* Author's collection

Richmond Hill, which offers a fascinating insight into life at the home for severely disabled ex-servicemen. There's even a short obituary for my grandfather who was there for a decade from the mid 1920s.

Of course newspapers and journals only offer a partial insight. There is much missing, although there is much more coverage from the 1850s when local papers really take off after the abolition of stamp duty. Also newspapers get things wrong (particularly names) and fail to follow stories up, so for example you may only get partial coverage of a trial.

The *Gentleman's Magazine*

For a century from 1731 the *Gentleman's Magazine* provided a way of confirming the births, marriages, and deaths of middle class and aristocratic families, as well as offering a fascinating insight into the world of Georgian England.

The original intention was to summarise the daily and weekly newspapers circulating in London "as a method much better calculated to preserve the things which are curious," much as *Reader's Digest* does today. Overtime more and more original material appeared within its pages, although a lot of it was dull and laboured poetry.

Most of the important stories of the day, events which we read about today in the history books, are reported. Yet they are often mentioned only in passing. The *Magazine*, for August 1776, contains the American Declaration of Independence perhaps the most important single document of the eighteenth century. Yet, it is printed next to an article about "Prince Ivan Alexis Knoutschoffschlerwitz" a Russian newly arrived in London who offered "his services to the ladies in the important business of their hairdressing" and provided a cure for baldness for gentlemen who "cannot submit to the gothic taste of covering their pates with wigs."

Each issue of the magazine to the mid-1830s is full of baptism, marriage and death notices, either gleaned from other newspapers or submitted by readers. Often the bare dates are supplemented by other information, which might not be found elsewhere. As might be expected entries for births are the least informative. Entries of marriages occasionally give more detail than just the names of the parties. In April 1776, the magazine reported the marriage of John Wilmot, eldest son of Sir John Eardley Wilmot to Miss Sainthill, "only daughter and heiress of the late Samuel Sainthill."

The *Gentleman's Magazine* is probably at its most useful with obituaries. Such as the one which appeared in July 1776 for Captain Gravener who died at Dover "He formerly commanded the York privateer and in 1745 drove a fleet of flat-bottomed boats on shore at Calais designed for an invasion." Ordinary people who were particularly old or remarkable were also covered. Another entry in July 1776 reported the death of Mrs Dorothy Clark at Westrope, Nottinghamshire aged 111 noting, "At 102 she reaped wheat against a man a whole day."

The National Archives Library, the Society of Genealogists and the Birmingham and Midlands Society for Heraldry and Genealogy have complete sets. Public and university libraries may have partial sets.

The first twenty years are online at www.bodley.ox.ac.uk/ilej. Many volumes are available on Google Books http://books.google.co.uk – this is probably the best place to start as there is a comprehensive index across all volumes. Access is free to both collections. And some volumes have been published on CD by the now defunct Archive CD Books and others.

Their genealogical worth has long been recognised. There are several indexes to marriages and obituaries, including Benjamin Nangle's *The Gentleman's Magazine: Biographical and Obituary Notices, 1781–1819 an index* (1980) and Edward Fry's *An Index to Marriages in the Gentleman's Magazine, 1731–1768* (1922).

Other reference books

There are other books which may contain references to your ancestors, particularly if they were reasonably well to do or famous. These books can be consulted in large public libraries, and include:

- *Oxford Dictionary of National Biography* – contains nearly 60,000 entries for famous (and not so famous) men and a few women. These entries are often very informative. If you are a member of a local library you can access this online; visit your council's website for details
- *Who's Who* – lists eminent (and frankly some less eminent) men and women of the day. When they die their entries are included in *Who was Who* which is published every decade or so. Again this should be available online via your local library
- *Burke's* and *Debrett's Peerage* contains details about nobility (including life peers), baronets, knights and on occasion landed gentry. The Society of Genealogists has runs of these volumes and its rivals. *Burke's Peerage* is available online (for a fee) at www.burkes-peerage.net

- There are dictionaries of biography of eminent personalities for many trades and professions. One of the best known is the *Dictionary of Labour Biography*, which includes biographies of activists in the labour movement. Many such dictionaries are online. For example a dictionary of scientific instrument makers is at www.sic.iuhps.org/in_bibli.htm

Online libraries

A surprising number of books have been digitised and available online. In general they are for books published before 1930. They may include old directories and transcriptions of old records or county histories mentioning the families in the county. The two largest collections are at:

- http://books.google.co.uk Google Books has scanned hundreds of thousands of books, but for copyright reasons often there is only a snippet showing the entry but not the context, which can limit its use
- www.gutenberg.org the Gutenberg Project has scanned in some 22,000 books, all of which are available for free

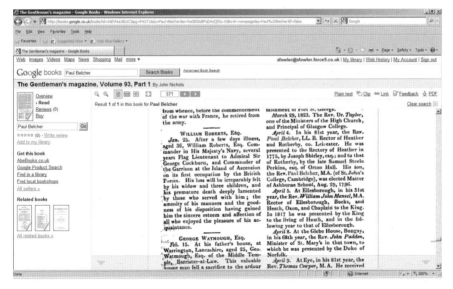

Google Books showing an entry for Paul Belcher in the Gentleman's Magazine.

Maps

Map making in Britain goes back to the sixteenth century. But for genealogists they only become interesting in the 1750s or thereabouts. Maps are useful because they show the places where our ancestors lived, so you can get an idea of the factory where they worked or the land which they farmed or fought over.

The most important series of maps are those produced by the Ordnance Survey from the first decade of the nineteenth century. These were the One Inch to One mile series of maps (generally referred to as the One-Inch maps) which have been produced ever since. Their direct descendents are the Landranger maps we might use for walking or driving today. These are small scale maps which do not show towns or villages in any great detail. For this you need the 2½-inch or 6-inch large scale series which will show individual buildings, fields and footpaths.

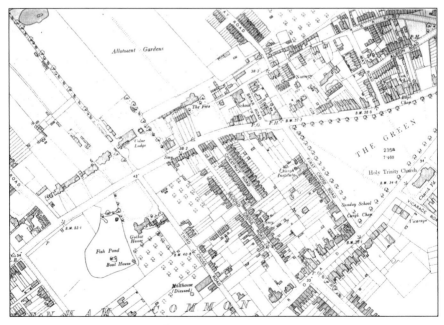

An extract from the six inch to the mile Ordnance Survey map for Twickenham published in 1894. Ordnance Survey / Alan Godfrey Maps

Series of old Ordnance Survey maps can be viewed online, although in many cases the quality is not high because the website owners want you to buy facsimiles from them. The best of these is: www.old-maps.co.uk. However reasonable quality sets of nineteenth century One-Inch maps can be viewed at www.visionofbritain.org.uk/maps and www.british-history.ac.uk/map.aspx. Fortunately facsimiles of both the One-Inch and many Six-Inch maps are readily available in bookshops, archives and museums at a very good price, so they are worth buying particularly if your ancestors always lived in a certain area. Look out for the excellent series of Cassini One-Inch maps (www.cassini maps.co.uk) and Alan Godfey maps of towns and neighbourhoods (www.alangodfreymaps.co.uk). The various series of Cassini maps show how Britain changed over 150 years, while most of Alan Godfrey are for towns as they appeared in about 1900.

There are four nationwide surveys which will be of interest if your ancestors were landowners or tenant farmers. Landowners in this instance might include families who only owned an acre or less. Largely because of the sheer numbers plus the difficulties of scanning large documents few of these maps have yet been digitised and placed online.

The enclosure of land took place in many rural parishes, particularly in southern England, during the eighteenth and nineteenth centuries. As part of the process maps (and accompanying schedules of property) were made to record the rearrangement of land ownership. The intention was to redistribute land to make larger and therefore more efficient fields. In the process many common lands were eradicated and local labourers suffered as a consequence. Maps and awards mostly at county record offices, but some are at The National Archives.

From the 1830s tithes (a tax paid by farmers to support the local clergy) were repealed or commuted. Tithe maps were drawn up to show the ownership of land in parishes. Several copies of these maps were made and normally one copy survives at The National Archives, while the other is at the local record office. There are also manuscript schedules which provide more details about who owned the land together with tenant farmers.

A detailed survey of land property was carried out by the Valuation Office between 1910 and 1915. If wasn't for the fact that the records created by the Office are fiendishly difficult to use they would be a natural supplement to the 1911 census. The maps are really adjutants to the notebooks which contain detailed descriptions of each property including number of rooms, out-houses and the like. Records are mostly at The National Archives but some records are at county record offices.

Now at The National Archives the National Farm Survey taken during the Secord World War is a detailed description of each farm and the crops grown and animals raised.

Further reading:
Geraldine Beech and Rose Mitchell, *Maps for Family Historians* (The National Archives, 2004)

Chapter 11

SCOTLAND AND IRELAND

S o many British people have Scottish and Irish ancestry (mine came from County Galway) that you may well need to use records from these countries. Each present their own challenges. Many Irish records were destroyed in a disastrous fire at the Four Courts Building in Dublin in 1922, while most Scottish records have little resemblance to their counterparts south of the border.

Scotland

Scottish records are very different to those you may become familiar with elsewhere in the British Isles, for two reasons – firstly the Presbyterian Church (rather than the Church of England) played a dominant role in Scottish life for centuries. In addition there is a unique legal tradition which

The home page for the Scotland's People website which is the key resource for tracing Scottish genealogy.

owes more to Europe than to London. That said it is actually very easy to get started because all the basic genealogical resources are available online at www.scotlandspeople.gov.uk. It is a pay to view site. And if you want to do research in person most of the important resources are available at the Scotland's People Centre off Princes Street in Edinburgh, which in turn is next door to the National Archives of Scotland.

These series of records are available through the Scotland's People website (or at the Centre if you choose to visit):

Statutory records of birth, marriage and death from 1855

A national system of birth, marriage and death registration was only adopted in Scotland in 1855. Before then events were imperfectly recorded in the Old Parish Registers (OPR) (See below).

A rather different system was adopted in Scotland than elsewhere in the British Isles, to start with there are no certificates. Instead you get access to the copy of the register which was compiled locally and sent to the General Register Office in Edinburgh. The registers for the first year, 1855, contain rather more information than for subsequent years. Protests about the amount of work these detailed requirements caused, led to a simplification in 1856 and subsequently. Even so the information on registers is, in general, rather more informative than their English equivalents.

INFORMATION ON REGISTERS FOR 1855 ONLY

- Birth registers: ages and birthplaces of the parents; number of other children, whether living or deceased
- Marriage registers: birth places of bride and groom; any children by former marriages whether living or deceased
- Death registers: place of birth of deceased; how long they had been living in the district where the death took place; the names and ages of any children living or deceased; place of burial, and the name of the undertaker

INFORMATION ON REGISTERS FROM 1856 (ITEMS NOT ON ENGLISH CERTIFICATES MARKED THUS*)

Births
- Surname and forename of the child
- Date and hour* of birth and the address where it took place
- Child's sex
- Father's name and his occupation (This would not be completed if the father was not known)
- Mother's name, with her maiden and former married names*
- The date and place of their marriage*
- Signature, designation and residence of the informant

Marriages
- Date and place of marriage. Unlike in England, marriages could take place outside the church or register office. Indeed marriage in church during the nineteenth century was rare. The usual location was the bride's home, but hotels were also popular
- Signatures of the parties*
- Their occupation, relationship if related*, and previous marital status
- Where they lived
- Names of fathers and mothers*, fathers' occupations
- Signature of officiating minister and two witnesses
- Date of registration and signature of registrar

Deaths
- Full name. If the surname had been changed then both names had to be stated
- Occupation, age and sex
- Whether single, married and widowed
- The name of any spouse
- Actual date and place including hour* of death
- Names and occupation of the parents of the deceased*
- The cause of death
- Signature and qualification of the informant

You can only search up to 1910 for baptisms, 1935 for marriages and 1960 for deaths on the Scotland's People website. More recent records must be consulted in person at the Scotland's People Centre in Edinburgh. New records are released each year: those for 1911, 1936 and 1961 respectively, for example, will be released in January 2012.

Census

Census returns are very similar to their English and Welsh equivalents. The first Scottish census was in 1801. Thereafter censuses have been taken every ten years, with the exception of 1941. Few if any records survive for the 1801 to 1831 censuses. Censuses are available between 1841 and 1901, although, as in England, the 1841 is not as useful as later ones. The 1911 census will become available in April 1911. Some censuses are also available online at ancestry.co.uk as well as through Scotland's People.

The layout of the form and the questions asked followed closely the English pattern. The only difference of note was the inclusion, in 1891, 1901 and 1911 of a question asking whether Gaelic was spoken in the household. Persons born in England were normally noted as having just been born in the country and it is reasonably rare to see the place of actual birth noted.

The census followed the English custom of calling women by their married names rather than the Scottish tradition of women retaining their maiden name on marriage. Some enumerators also anglicised forenames, for example calling women Jane rather than the Scots Jean or Janet rather than Jessie.

Old Parish Registers (OPRs)

Before the introduction of civil registration in 1855, the parish ministers or session clerks of Church of Scotland parishes kept these registers, which record births and baptisms, proclamation of banns and marriages, and deaths and burials. However, they are far from complete. The oldest register is baptisms and banns at Errol, Perthshire which dates from 1553, for many parishes the earliest registers are only for the early nineteenth century. The reasons for this incompleteness are manyfold, but include the fact that by the late eighteenth century increasing numbers of people were turning away from the established church to other denominations and that, on occasion, a fee was charged. In addition standards of record keeping vary considerably

WHAT THE OLD PARISH REGISTERS MAY TELL YOU

Baptisms
Most registers should contain the following information:

- Date of the baptism, often with the date of birth
- Name of father and mother (often with her maiden name)
- In earlier registers, it is common to include names of witnesses with their occupations
- Illegitimacy is usually referred to as 'born in fornication' and the name of the father, where known, is noted

Marriages
The information recorded in registers of marriages and banns are usually very sparse and normally only record:

- Date of the event
- Names of both spouses
- Occasionally the name of the bride's father

and most entries contain very little information. That said, there is a comprehensive index to baptisms and marriages online at www.scotlands people.gov.uk. The website also has entries from registers and other records kept by Catholic parishes between 1703 and 1908.

DEATHS

Finding the death or burial of an individual is particularly frustrating. The OPR entries for deaths vary greatly. Indeed, in Scott on occasion, they may be little more than accounts of people borrowing the mort-cloth used in the funeral ceremony. To an extent this can be overcome by using monumental inscriptions. A large collection of these monumental inscriptions is at New Register House. Local studies libraries may have sets for their area, although there are few lists of Scottish monumental inscriptions at the Society of Genealogists.

An entry from the Register from Fordyce recording the birth of Alexander Calder in 1821. General Register Office for Scotland

Wills, testaments and inventories

The big difference between wills and their Scottish equivalents – testaments – is that testaments are restricted to moveable property. Heritable property, that is land and buildings are covered by retours or services of heirs. These records are easy to use, because they are indexed, in good condition, and fairly easy to read.

Technically these records are the confirmations of appointment of executor to administer the moveable property of the deceased, whether he or she made a will or not. Each testament gives the name of the deceased, usually the date of death, the confirmation of the executor, and inventory (or list) of the moveable property of the deceased (which may include household furniture, implements of trade, and debts owed to and by the deceased). There may also be a copy of the will itself.

Up to 1822 all testaments were confirmed by regional ecclesiastical Commissary Courts. From 1823 this work was taken over by the Sheriff Courts. Each court undertook their business in slightly different ways.

The wills and testaments index on the Scotlandspeople website has over 600,000 index entries to wills and testaments from 1513 to 1901. Each index entry lists the surname, forename, title, occupation and place of residence (where these are given) of the deceased person, the court in which the testament was recorded, with the date. Index entries do not include names of executors, trustees or heirs to the estate. They also do not include the deceased's date of death, or the value of the estate.

If you are searching for a will or testament, you should bear in mind that there was no legal requirement for individuals to make a will. Indeed, comparatively few people actually bothered. Even if someone died intestate, there was no obligation for the family to go to court to have the deceased's affairs settled. Families generally sorted things out amicably amongst themselves, in which case there will be no testament.

However, it is always worthwhile checking the indexes, because they can include persons from quite humble origins.

Sometimes the intervention of the court to settle the deceased's affairs was not required until many years after the death, possibly due to a dispute, therefore if a will or testament exists, it may be recorded much later than might be expected.

As well as the index images of the documents are also available here. These images are full colour, authentic facsimiles of the original documents at the National Archives of Scotland

Other resources

Not everything is yet online. The National Archives of Scotland, in particular, has many records which could help once you have exhausted the resources of Scotlandspeople. Their holdings include much unique material, such as:

- **Retours, or Service of Heirs** – until 1868 land or buildings – known as heritable property – could not be left in a will. Inheritances of this type of property was recorded in the Retours, or Services of Heirs. Other details to be found are the names of the heir and the deceased, their relationship, and possibly the date of death. Retours begin in 1547, and were written in Latin until 1847. The originals are at the NAS, although indexes may be found in large reference libraries in Scotland
- **Sasines** – registers of sasines record the transfer of land and houses from 1617. There is no English equivalent. If your ancestors owned even the

smallest piece of land, or cottage, you should find something in these registers. The bequest of land within families may help you establish family relationships. Even if no family links are established there will be information about the location of the property, the size of any land, and the occupations of the vendor and purchaser

Most sasines are at the NAS, but registers, for Aberdeen, Dundee (both before 1809) and Glasgow, are held by local record offices. The Society of Genealogists has copies of a few indexes to burgh registers of sasines.

- **Kirk Session Records** – each Church of Scotland parish had its own Kirk Session, which administered the affairs of the parish. This covered most aspects of people's lives, a great deal of information can be found in Session Books, such as the misconduct of parishioners on the Sabbath – particularly for fornication. These records also deal with the relief offered

The Hawick Hub houses the Scottish Borders Archives in a splendid new building. Scottish Borders Council

poor members of the parish, the appointment of school masters and other employees, and the loan of burial clothes. Many Session Books are at the NAS, while others are at local record offices. A number have been transcribed and published

Often forgotten by family historians outside the country, there is a network of smaller archives and local history libraries across Scotland which often have the statutory records, censuses and OPRs for their areas on microfilm plus local newspapers and photographs, and much beside. The largest is Glasgow's Mitchell Library which is a huge resource for anybody whose ancestors came from Glasgow or indeed Strathclyde as a whole: Mitchell Library, 201 North Street, Glasgow G3 7DN, tel 0141 287 2872; www.mitchelllibrary.org. The National Library of Scotland also has many records. Of particular note is the extensive collection of digitised maps of the country at www.nls.uk/maps

Further reading:
For some strange reason there are a plethora of books about researching Scottish family history. They all seem to be of a high standard, these are the most recent:

Bruce Drurie, *Scottish Genealogy* (The History Press, 2009)
Graham Holton and Jack Winch, *Discover Your Scottish Ancestry: Internet and Traditional Resources* (Edinburgh University Press, 2009)
Ian Maxwell, *Tracing Your Scottish Ancestors* (Pen & Sword, 2009)
Chris Paton, *Researching Scottish Family History* (Family History Partnership, 2010)
Cecil Sinclair, *Jock Tamson's Bairns* (GROS, 2000) – explains why and how the records were created
Cecil Sinclair, *Tracing Your Scottish Ancestors* (4th edn, National Archives of Scotland, 2009)

Irish research

Most of your research into your Irish ancestors will naturally have to be undertaken in Ireland as relatively little is yet online, although, there are increasing number of websites, books and CDs which can help you before you arrive.

Tracing Irish ancestry is complicated by two factors:

- For the vast majority of the population very few records were kept until the middle of the nineteenth century
- A fire at the Fours Courts destroyed much irreplaceable material during the Irish Civil War in 1922

As a result it is sometimes said that it is impossible to trace Irish ancestors. This is not really true, but it is not always as simple as it might be.

The Irish administrative tradition is similar to that of England, which means most of the records are very similar to records used in researching English ancestry. In particular births, marriage and death certificates and census returns are virtually identical. Apart from a few early legal documents and some Catholic parish registers, which may be in Latin, the records are likely to be in English.

Much of your research can be done in Dublin, although you might need to visit Belfast if your ancestors came from Northern Ireland. In addition most counties, north as well as south, has one or more family history or heritage centres with a range of local material. There may also be county or city archives which can help. Details of most libraries are at www.askaboutireland.ie.

Civil registration

The Irish system of civil registration formally began on 1 January 1864. However, between 1 April 1845 and 31 December 1863, non-Roman Catholics had to register their marriages with the authorities.

The records are held at General Register offices in Roscommon (with a public reading room in Dublin) and Belfast. In the south there are birth, marriage and death certificates 1864–1922 all Ireland; 1922 to date Irish Free State/Republic of Ireland. And in Belfast (for the six counties of Northern Ireland only): births, marriages and deaths 1864 to date.

The system of getting access to the certificates is very similar to that in England and Wales. In Dublin a fee to search the registers, currently €20, is charged per day. Individual certificates cost €10.

In Belfast certificates currently cost £12; no fee is charged for searching the registers.

The LDS Church (Mormons) has microfilm copies of some indexes up to 1957 which can be consulted at their family history centres.

In addition GROs in Belfast and Dublin have the appropriate registers relating to maritime, consular and military births, marriages and deaths.

The information given on certificates is very similar to their English equivalents.

Censuses

Censuses have been held in Ireland every ten years since 1821. Unfortunately few records survive before 1901. The surviving records are either at PRONI (for Northern Ireland) or the National Archives (all-Ireland).

Usefully the 1901 and 1911 survive and are now online at www.census.nationalarchives.ie. This is a free service and is excellent. The information on these records is very similar to that found on English returns, although in 1901 and 1911 householders are asked to state whether individuals can read and write, about the length of their marriage, or whether they can speak Irish.

The census return for John Darcy and his family who were grocers in Clifden, County Galway.
National Archives of Ireland

Parish registers

Roman Catholic

As the Roman Catholic faith was illegal until 1778 and then tolerated until 1829, there are few Catholic parish registers before the 1820s. They are almost entirely for baptisms and marriages, though death or funeral entries occur occasionally. Baptism entries do, however, include the names of sponsors and the names of witnesses.

Most parish registers before 1880 have been microfilmed by the National Library of Ireland. After this date they are often with the parish priest. The microfilm copies of the registers can be consulted at the Library, although PRONI has copies relating to the six counties and border areas in the Republic. Copies of some registers are at the SoG.

Church of Ireland

In 1560 the Anglican Church of Ireland became the established church in Ireland. Unlike its sister church in England it never had the support of the majority of the population. The majority of registers begin during the eighteenth century, but were destroyed in 1922. Surviving records are either with the parish, at the National Archives, PRONI (for Northern Ireland), or with the Representative Church Body Library. Again microfilm copies of some parish registers may be in the SoG Library.

Nonconformists

Various non conformist sects established themselves in Ireland (particularly in the north) during the seventeenth and eighteenth centuries. As the authorities looked on them suspiciously their parish registers tend not to begin much before the 1840s. Surviving records are kept by the church itself or at the PRONI in Belfast.

Wills and testaments

The system of administration of probate was very similar to that in England. It should however be remembered that most people were too poor to leave a will, so that the records discussed below are largely for the Anglo-Irish landowners and merchants in the larger towns.

Before 1858 wills were proved in a court of the Church of Ireland. The most important of which was Prerogative Court of Armagh. Each diocese also had its own consistory court dealing with less important wills. In 1858 a national and secular probate register was established in Dublin, along English lines, to administer wills.

Much of the pre-1857 material, as well as wills proved under the new system to 1900, were lost in the Four Courts fire. However, some indexes survive which can contain useful genealogical information.

The National Archives has surviving records before 1922, as well as wills proved between 1922 and 1982 for the Irish Republic.

PRONI has records of the district registries for Belfast, Armagh and Londonderry, between 1900 and 1986 (Armagh 1900–1921 only). An index is at www.proni.gov.uk/index/search_the_archives/will_calendars/wills_search

Other sources

Many directories and other records have been digitised and made available on compact discs by Eneclann, details at www.eneclann.ie.

Directories

The first trade and street directories were published for Dublin in 1751. The most important of these directories was Thom's, which also included details of official appointments. The National Archives Library at Kew has a run of Thom's between 1844 and 1928. The SoG also has a number of directories, the earliest dating from 1761. In Dublin, both the National Archives and the National Library have sets, while in Belfast copies of directories particularly for the six counties are at PRONI: see www.proni.gov.uk/index/search_the_archives/street_directories.htm

Maps

The first detailed maps of Ireland were drawn up during the 1830s and early 1840s in order to show land ownership as part of the introduction of a new land tax. Townland maps on a scale of six inches to one mile were completed for the whole country by 1842. This massive undertaking ensured that the island was surveyed with a degree of thoroughness and accuracy unique for its time. The completed maps show Ireland as it was just before the ravages of the Famine. The largest collection of maps in Ireland is at the National Library – www.nli.ie/en/printed-maps-introduction.aspx. PRONI has many maps for Northern Ireland. Many are also online at www.pasthomes.com and www.irishhistoricmaps.ie

202   STREET DIRECTORY.

23 Lewis Scott, stonecutter
25 Alex. Boyd, moulder
27 David Taggart, storekeeper
29 & 31 James Stephenson, grocer
33 Samuel M'Conkey, grocer
35 James Campbell, linen-lapper
37 James M'Neilly, porter
39 Mrs. A. Galway
41 Gateway
43 James Hill, baker
45 Edward Lynn, bootmaker
47 Mrs. Scott
49 Hans Beatty
    Vacant ground
63 George Butler, pensioner
65 John Crozier, warper
67 Samuel Vance, clerk
69 Mrs. Haslett
71 James Melvin, mechanic
73 Robert Innis
75 Stewart M'Kee, grocer
77 George Telford
79 James Campbell
81 Mrs. Donnelly, side door
80 Wm. M'Conbrey, carter
78 Wm, Taylor, grocer
76 George Williamson
74 John Smylie, ironturner
72 Nathaniel Rodgers
70 Alex. M'Clurg, porter
68 Hugh Montgomery
66 Thomas Mulholland, local-constable
64 Robert Mulholland, carpenter
62 John M'Cullough
60 North Boundary Street brass-foundry; J. & S. Cott, proprietors
    Vacant ground
44 Francis Robinson, grocer
42 George Liggett, local-constable
40 John M'Bratney, dealer
38 James Thorpe, brushmaker
36 Henry Hunt, shoemaker
34 George Whitla, clerk
,, E. Whitla, dressmaker
32 Robert Hunt, baker
30 Mrs. M'Ardle
28 Wm. J. Harper, porter
26 Henry Hasson, pensioner
24 Samuel Neill, breadserver
22 Wm. Hamill, painter
20 Mrs. Pearson, mangler
18 Mrs. Dillon
16 Francis Hyde, flaxdresser
14 Eliza Suiter

12 Wm. M'Curdy, carpenter
10 Abraham Neill, local-constable
8 James Riddell, reedmaker
    Samuel Keatley, pawn-office (side doors)

Northburn Court.
Off Leadbetter-street.
Four small houses

Northburn Place.
(See Old Lodge Road.)

North Queen Place.
Off Albert-street.
Twenty-four small houses

North Queen Street Place.
Off North Queen-street.
Six small houses

North Queen Street.
Donegall-street to Spamount.
1 Belfast Mercantile Academy; J. Pyper, principal
3 —— M'Kibbin, local-constable
5 George Maxwell, confectionery
7 & 9 Robert Irwin, side door
11 Charles Collins, labourer
13 Samuel Green, shoemaker
15 James Thomson, flesher
17 David Long, foundry-worker
19 North Queen Street Constabulary Station
21 & 23 Mrs. M'Millan
25 J. Blair, tailor
27 Michael Mansfield, dealer
29 Peter Salmon, slater
31 John Allen, lodging-house
33 Patrick Duprey, sawyer
35 James Hanna, foundry-worker
37 Polly Warton
39 Wm. M'Comb, publican
41 John Johnston, stonecutter
43 Bernard M'Teak, dealer
45 Robert Brown, clerk
47 Vacant
49 Robert Ireland, greengrocer
51 John White, publican
53 Patrick Cheevers, publican
55 Wm. Frame
,, Mrs. M. Thompson, grocer
57 & 59 Wm. Horner, dealer
61 Wm. Egan, dealer
63 Gibbs Entry door
65 Patrick Farrelly

STREET DIRECTORY.   203

67 & 69 J. O'Connor, publican
71 & 73 John Kenny, pensioner
75 Mrs. Boyd
77 Wm. M'Donald, shoemaker
79 Jane Willasey, dealer
81 Wm. Caplin, dealer
83 Margaret Lynn, grocer
85 John Houston, yarnbundler
87 Vacant
89 Kirker, Brothers, bakery and flour store
91 Mrs. Gilmore, haberdasher and milliner
93 James Bryan, haberdasher
95 Samuel Lawther; office, Corporation Street
97 Thomas Price, notary public, commissioner for taking affidavits, and commission agent
99 Robert Godbey, clerk
105 Edward Smith, spirit-dealer
107 & 109 John Canavan, grocer and spirit-dealer
111 Edward M'Stay, reeling-master
113 Mrs. Heaney
115 Crawford J. Tully, spirit-dealer
117 & 119 Clements Fitzgerald, grocer
121 Vacant
123 Abel Hadskis, pawnbroker
    Vacant ground
131 John M'Gurk, shipcarpenter
133 Thomas Fullerton, clerk
135 Christopher O'Neill, clerk
137 James Gribben, schoolmaster
139 Mrs. Kirk
141 John Forsythe, pensioner
143 Hamilton Anderson, clerk
145 Archibald M'Fall, clerk
    Garden Hill—Wm. Thompson, secretary, Belfast Harbour-office
    James M'Keown
94 Mrs. M'Quillan, dealer
92 Bernard King, publican
90 Fox Tavern—A. M. Lester, proprietor
88 Thomas Colgan, grocer
86 Wm. Montgomery, shoemaker
84 Owen Dougherty, dealer
82 Vacant
80 Alice M'Guigan, dealer
78 Mrs. Shane, dressmaker
76 Joseph Finlay, grocer and publican
74 Wm. Orr, grocer

72 James M'Cann, shoemaker and greengrocer
70 Patrick Dogherty, dealer
64 R. T. Hilland, grocer
62 Arthur Gamble, pawnbroker
    Cavalry barracks and entrance
60 & 58 T. M'Gurk, spirit-dealer
56 Alex. K. Burke, tailor
52 Wm. Rodgers, livery yard
50½ Margaret Murray, fruiterer
50 Occupied by soldiers
48 & 46 Wm. Cosgrove, haberdasher
44 Vacant
42 Mrs. Craigon
40 Mrs. Pascoe
38 Robert Brown, collector of tax and professor of music
36 Entry door
34 Richard Gardner, clerk
32 & 30 Vacant
28 Charles Frost, agent
26 & 24 Yards
22 Mrs. Knox
20 Lieut. Boyd, 63rd Regt.
18 Mrs. Murphy
16 & 14 Thomas Boyd, bakery and flour stores
12 Vacant
10 Vacant
8 Thomas Anderson; pawnoffice, Lancaster Street
6 John M'Clinton, of M'Clinton & Thompson, 53 & 55, Academy Street
4 James Cameron
2 Mrs. Dyer, shop; John Street
    Old Poor House—Robert Gill, housesteward; Wm. Vance, schoolmaster; Miss J. Brown, matron; Miss M. Anderson, schoolmistress; D. Whaley, gatekeeper

North King Street.
Brown-square to Gardiner-street.
1 Wm. Hull, labourer
3 David Dalton, porter
5 Robert Davis, nailer
7 Wm. Curry, labourer
9 Nathaniel Lawther, labourer
11 Wm. M'Kendry, seaman
13 G. Gregg, cardriver
15 Robert Miller, carter
14 James M'Millen
12 Robert Thompson, labourer

A page from the Belfast and Ulster Directory 1863–1864. Public Record Office of Northern Ireland

Records specific to Ireland

There are a number of specifically Irish records which can be used to flesh out other sources. They are largely to do with property, which usually excludes the mass of the population who were either landless labourers or small tenant farmers.

The Primary Valuation of Ireland – Griffith's Valuation – was a survey of land and property carried out between 1846 and 1865 by Sir Richard Griffith.

The National Library of Ireland has many resources for family historians including a Genealogy Advisory Service and the Office of the Chief Herald. Irish Tourist Board

Its purpose was to establish a means by which a tax could be calculated for the upkeep of the poor. The survey lists names of landowners and tenants, together with the extent and value of their property. About 1.25m people appear in these records, so the valuation can to an extent be used as a replacement for the missing census records, although only the name of the landowner or tenant is given. Copies are available at the National Archives and PRONI (for Northern Ireland) and online at www.askaboutireland.ie/ griffith-valuation/index.xml and www.irisiorigins.com. The indexes may also help you identify the place where a person was born, which in turn will help track down parish registers.

Subsequent valuations of property from 1846 in the Irish Republic have been administered by the Valuation Office. Their records are open to inspection on the payment of a fee. For individual properties these registers will tell you the occupier's name, acreage of the property, and its rateable value. Their address is Valuation Office, Irish Life Centre, Abbey St Lower, Dublin 1; www.valoff.ie The equivalent records for Northern Ireland are at PRONI.

Tithe Applotment Books
Between 1823 and 1838 tithe applotment books were compiled to access the level of tithes to be paid to the Church of Ireland. This survey identified all landowners and the amount that he owned, together with the crops grown and the quality of land farmed. The books however are by no means complete as some parishes were too poor for tithes to be levied. These records are at the National Archives, with copies for Northern Ireland at PRONI. Indexes are online at www.ancestry.co.uk.

Further reading:
Anthony Adolph, *Collins Tracing Your Irish Family History* (Collins, 2007)
John Grenham, *Tracing your Irish Family History* (Gill & Macmillan, 2006)
Ian Maxwell, *Tracing Your Irish Ancestors* (Pen & Sword, 2009)
Ian Maxwell, *Tracing Your Northern Irish Ancestors* (Pen & Sword, 2010)

FIRST INFORMATION ABOUT AN INDIVIDUAL

Introduction

Use this form to jot down what you already know about a member of your family and what you need to find out. The more information you have the better, but don't worry if there are lots of blank spaces, we have all got to start somewhere. You may find that you know more about an individual than you think you do. Ask other relatives to see whether they can help fill in the gaps.

Please feel free to amend the sheet as necessary – it is there to jog the memory rather than as a straitjacket.

Name: _____

Date of birth: _____ Date of death: _____ Date of marriage: _____

How is she/he related to you? _____

Name of wife/husband 1: _____

Dates of their birth/death: _____ Date of marriage: _____

Name of wife/husband 2: _____

Dates of their birth/death: _____

Children (with dates of birth and death)

1: _____

2: _____

3: _____

4: _____

5: _____

6: _____

How they earned their money? _____

Military Service? (if yes, which service): _____

Address(es) where they lived: _____

_____

_____

_____

_____

_____

FURTHER READING

There are hundreds of books on family history. And despite the internet they continue to be published in large numbers (bizarrely some of the most popular are basically lists of websites). Most bookshops often have very general introductory texts which are often woefully out of date – exceptions are the specialist bookshops at the Society of Genealogists and The National Archives which have most of the family history books in print. However, if you don't live in London you can buy books online either direct from the publisher or at www.amazon.co.uk. Out of print books can also be bought via abebooks at www.abebooks.co.uk.

There are many general introductory titles, few of which I would recommend, as they tend to be both expensive and inaccurate. Exceptions are:

- Mark D Herber, *Ancestral Trails* (2nd edition, Sutton, 2005)
- Pauline Saul, *The Family Historians Enquire Within* (FFHS, 1995) – a new edition by Paul Gaskell for the Family History Partnership is due out in 2011

Also worth looking at are the series of books by Anthony Adolph for Collins, and Robert Blatchford's *Family and Local History Handbook* (published annually by Robert Blatchford Publishing).

A range of more specialist titles are published by Pen & Sword, The National Archives the Society of Genealogist, the Family History Partnership and Countryside Books. They are worth buying if you want to investigate a particular aspect of your family history, such as careers of men in the armed forces.

Pen & Sword (www.pen-and-sword.co.uk)
Pen & Sword have been publishing specialist family books since 2007. I have written several titles in the series as well as providing editorial help. About half a dozen new titles are published each year.

Nick Barratt, *Nick Barratt's Guide To Your Ancestors' Lives* (2010)
Rachel Bellerby, *Tracing your Yorkshire Ancestors* (2006)
Gill Blanchard, *Tracing Your East Anglian Ancestors* (2009)
Geoff Bridger, *The Great War Handbook A Guide for Family Historians & Students of the Conflict* (2009)
Richard Brooks and Matthew Little, *Royal Marine Ancestors* (2008)
Robert Burlison, *Tracing Your Pauper Ancestors* (2009)
Anthony Burton, *Tracing Your Shipbuilding Ancestors* (2010)
Mark Crail, *Tracing Your Labour Movement Ancestors* (2009)
Di Drummond, *Tracing your Railway Ancestors* (2010)
Brian Elliott, *Tracing Your Coalmining Ancestors* (2011)
Simon Fowler, *Researching Military History Online* (2007)
Simon Fowler, *Tracing Your Army Ancestors* (2006)
Simon Fowler, *Tracing Your Naval Ancestors* (2011)
Keith Gregson, *Tracing Your Northern Ancestors* (2007)
Ian Maxwell, *Tracing Your Irish Ancestors* (2008)
Ian Maxwell, *Tracing Your Northern Irish Ancestors* (2010)
Ian Maxwell, *Tracing Your Scottish Ancestors* (2009)
Mike Royden, *Tracing Your Liverpool Ancestors* (2010)
Vivian Teasdale, *Tracing Your Textile Ancestors* (2008)
Phil Tomaselli, *Tracing your Air Force Ancestors* (2007)
Phil Tomaselli, *Tracing Your Secret Service Ancestors* (2009)
Stephen Wade, *Tracing Your Police Ancestors* (2009)
Stephen Wade, *Tracing Your Criminal Ancestors* (2009)
Rosemary Wenzerul, *Tracing your Jewish Ancestors* (2008)
Martin Wilcox, *Fishing and Fishermen* (2008)

The National Archives (www.nationalarchives.gov.uk/bookshop)
Over the years The National Archives (and before it the Public Record Office) has published many excellent guides. They no longer publish books, but you should still be able to find these titles in bookshops and libraries. In particular you should consider buying Amanda Bevan and Peter Christian's books as they are the best in the field.

David Annal, *Easy Family History* (2006)
Amanda Bevan, *Tracing your Ancestors at The National Archives* (7th edition, 2006)
Peter Christian, *The Genealogists Internet* (4th edition, 2007)

Simon Fowler, *Workhouse: the people, the places, life behind closed doors* (2008)
Michael Gandy, *Family History Cultures and Faiths* (2007)
Roger Kershaw, *Family history on the move* (2006)
Mark Pearsall, *Family History Companion* (2007)
Bruno Pappalardo, *Tracing Your Naval Ancestors* (2003)
Chris Pomery, *Family History in the Genes: trace your DNA and grow your family tree* (2007)
William Spencer, *Air Force Records: a guide for family historians* (2008)
William Spencer, *Army Records: a guide for family historians* (2008)
William Spencer, *Family history in the wars* (2007)
William Spencer, *Medals: the researcher's guide* (2008)

Society of Genealogists (www.sog.org.uk)
The Society has been publishing books for many years. Their titles are generally very good, but can be hard to track down because they only print small numbers and it is sometimes difficult to discover what is in print. Current titles are listed on their website.

Family History Partnership (www.familyhistorypartnership.co.uk)
The Partnership arose out of the collapse of the Federation of Family History Society's publishing programme a few years ago. They have taken over most of the titles published by the Society – including the well-known Gibson Guides – and are now publishing new titles. Again a full list can be found on their website.

Countryside Books (www.countrysidebooks.co.uk)
Publish a small number of family history books including:

Simon Fowler, *Tracing your First World War Ancestors* (2nd edition, 2009)
Simon Fowler, *Tracing your Second World War Ancestors* (2005)
Charles Masters, *Essential Maps for Family Historians* (2009)
Jayne Shrimpton, *Book Details: Family Photographs and How to Date Them* (2008)
Neil Storey, *Military Photographs & How to Date Them* (2009)
John Titford, *Writing Up Your Family History* (2006)
Margaret Ward, *The Female Line* (2006)
Margaret Ward, *Female Occupations – Women's Employment 1850–1950* (2008)

Magazines

Perhaps surprisingly there are six magazines published for family historians. You should be able to find them in branches of WH Smith and larger supermarkets. They all contain articles for beginners plus a range of features on ancestors' lives and using computers and the internet in your research. They are also a good way of keeping up with developments in the hobby such as the arrival of material online or the release of new records. I have a soft spot for *Family History Monthly*, which I once edited, but frankly they are all much of a muchness so choose one which you feel comfortable with.

Compact discs and microfilm

Hundreds of CDs (compact discs) have been published generally containing facsimiles of books which are no longer in print or datasets which can be interrogated by the user. Increasingly they are being superseded by resources online, but they sometimes can still be useful. The largest publisher is S&N Genealogy Supplies, whose catalogue is at www.genealogysupplies.com. Most local family history societies also publish material on CD. You may occasionally come across reference to discs published by Archive CD Books which unfortunately ceased publishing a few years ago.

Even more obsolete than CDs are microfilm and microfiche copies of records (or microform). You may well have to use records in this form when visiting local record offices. Even The National Archives still has collections of material available only on microfilm, although this is rapidly decreasing. They can be tricky to use and the images hard to read. Unless you are a complete technophobe, online equivalents are incomparably better. Occasionally family history societies still publish datasets on microfilm or microfiche.

USEFUL ADDRESSES

These are the addresses for the major archives and libraries that you might use in your research, most of which are mentioned elsewhere in the book. It is not comprehensive as it is fairly easy to find details of local or specialist archives and libraries online, which in any case is more likely to be up-to-date.

National institutions

British Library, 96 Euston Road, London NW1 2DB; Tel: 020 7412 7000, www.bl.uk

British Library Newspapers, Colindale Avenue, London NW9 5HE, telephone 020 7412 7353, www.bl.uk. The Library will close during 2012 and the resources moved to the main British Library site

British Postal Museum and Archives, Freeling House, Phoenix Place, London WC1X 0DL; http://postalheritage.org.uk

BT Archives, Third Floor Holborn Telephone Exchange, 268–270 High Holborn London WC1V 7EE; www.btplc.com/thegroup/btshistory/btgrouparchives

Catholic National Library, St Michael's Abbey, Farnborough Road, Farnborough GU14 7NQ; www.catholic-library.org.uk

Commonwealth War Graves Commission, 2 Marlow Road, Maidenhead SL6 7DX, tel 01628 507200, www.cwgc.org

The National Archives, Ruskin Avenue, Kew, Richmond TW9 4DU; tel 020 8876 3444, www.nationalarchives.gov.uk

National Library of Wales, Aberystwyth SY23 3BU; tel 01970 632 800, www.llgc.org.uk

National Monuments Record, Kemble Drive, Swindon SN2 2GZ; tel: 01793 414600, www.english-heritage.org.uk/nmr

Military museums and archives

Army Museums Ogilby Trust – www.armymuseums.org.uk has details of all local regimental museums

Fleet Air Arm Museum, RNAS Yeovilton, Ilchester BA22 8HT, tel 01935 840565, www.fleetairarm.com

Imperial War Museum, Lambeth Road, London SE1 6HZ, tel 020 7334 3922, www.iwm.org.uk. The URL for the collections database is www.iwm collections.org.uk

National Army Museum, Royal Hospital Road, London SW34 HT; tel 020 7730 0717, www.national-army-museum.org.uk

National Maritime Museum, Romney Road, Greenwich, London SE10 9NF; tel 020 8312 6565, www.nmm.ac.uk

RAF Museum, Graeme Park Way, London NW9 5LL, tel 020 8295 2266, www.rafmuseum.org.uk

Royal Marines Museum, Southsea PO4 9PX, tel: 023 9281 9385, www. royalmarinesmuseum.co.uk

Royal Naval Museum, H M Naval Base, Portsmouth PO1 3NH; tel 023 9272 7562, www.royalnavalmuseum.org

Family history resources

Federation of Family History Societies, PO Box 8857, Lutterworth LE17 9BJ; tel 01455 203133, www.ffhs.org.uk

General Register Office, PO Box 2, Southport PR8 2JD; tel 0845 603 7788, www.gro.gov.uk/gro/content/certificates

Institute of Heraldic and Genealogical Studies, 79–81 Northgate, Canterbury CT1 1BA, tel 01227 768664, www.ihgs.ac.uk

London Family History Centre, 64–68 Exhibition Road, London SW7 2PA; tel 020 7589 8561, www.londonfhc.org

Society of Genealogists, 14 Charterhouse Buildings, Goswell Road, London EC1M 7BA; tel: 020 7251 8799, www.sog.org.uk

Archives and libraries

www.nationalarchives.gov.uk/archon has details of all local record offices, local studies libraries and most specialist archives across the United Kingdom (and often further afield)

Scotland

General Register Office for Scotland, HM General Register House, 2 Princes Street, Edinburgh EH1 3Y; www.gro-scotland.gov.uk

National Archives of Scotland, HM General Register House, Edinburgh EH1 3YY; tel 0131–535 1334, www.nas.gov.uk

National Library of Scotland, 57 George IV Bridge, Edinburgh EH1 1EW; tel
    0131 623 3700, www.nls.uk
Scotland's People Centre, HM General Register House, 2 Princes Street,
    Edinburgh EH1 3YY; tel 0131 314 4300, www.scotlandspeoplehub.gov.uk.
    A day ticket costs £10
Scottish Genealogy Society, 15 Victoria Terrace, Edinburgh, EH1 2JL, tel 0131
    220 3677, www.scotsgenealogy.com

Ireland
To ring numbers in the Irish Republic from Britain add the international
prefix 353 and omit the initial 0 in the dialling code.

National Archives of Ireland, Bishops St, Dublin 8; tel 01 407 2300,
    www.nationalarchives.ie
National Library of Ireland, Kildare St, Dublin 2; tel 01 603 0200, www.nli.ie
General Register Office, Government Offices, Convent Road, Roscommon;
    tel 090 663 2900, www.groireland.ie. There is a public reading room where
    the indexes can be consulted in person – 3rd Floor, Block 7, Irish Life Centre,
    Lower Abbey Street, Dublin 1. A day ticket costs € 20.
Dublin City Archives, 138 – 144 Pearse Street, Dublin 2; tel 01 674 4999,
    www.dublincity.ie
Representative Church Body Library, Braemor Park, Rathgar, Dublin 14;
    01 492 3979, www.ireland.anglican.org / library
Public Record Office of Northern Ireland (PRONI), 66 Balmoral Ave, Belfast
    BT9 6NY; tel 028 9025 5905, www.proni.gov.uk. PRONI is moving to new
    premises in Belfast's Titanic Quarter in the late spring of 2011. Full details
    are available on its website
General Register Office of Northern Ireland, Oxford House, 49–55 Chichester
    St, Belfast BT1 4HL, tel 028 9025 2000; www.groni.gov.uk
Ulster Historical Foundation, 49 Malone Road, Belfast BT9 6RY; tel 028 9066
    1988, www.ancestryireland.com

Appendix IV

HOW TO READ A DOCUMENT

Unless you go back much before the middle of the eighteenth century you should not have much difficulty in reading old documents. However, if you get stuck these hints might help:

Enlarge the document
Wherever possible, make a copy of the document and try to enlarge it, using a scanner. It is always easier to work with a document if you are able to touch and mark, and also it is much easier to read individual letters and words when they are larger.

Put together an alphabet
Whatever type of hand (or style of writing) you are trying to read, do not give in to hasty guesswork as this can lead to all kinds of problems further along the line. The best place to start when faced with a new document is to put together an alphabet for yourself. By doing this, you will find that more and more of the words become clear.

Pick out the words you definitely know and use these to get an example of as many letters as you can. For some documents you will need a list of capital letters too, as sometimes these are quite different to their lower-case equivalents. An alphabet will also allow you to distinguish between letters which look similar to each other, which is one of the most difficult problems you will encounter.

Confusing letters to watch out for are:
c and r; s and f; n, m, i, u and v

Other tips
Understanding the background to the document will help enormously with reading the handwriting. Many types of documents contain standard phrases or formulae. It is much harder to read a document if you do not know what kind of document it is. If you know the phrases which are likely to appear, you will be able to read them more easily when they appear. You can also use them to help decipher other words.

Be prepared to tackle an old document letter by letter if necessary. If you can't work out what a letter is, do a few more lines and go back and see if you can identify it then.

Taking it further

If you want to practice getting to know old handwriting, The National Archives has an excellent online tutorial at www.nationalarchives.gov.uk/palaeography.

Hilary Marshall, *Palaeography for Family and Local Historians* (Phillimore, 2004)

DRAWING UP A FAMILY TREE

O ne of the aims of family history is ultimately to draw up a chart which shows your ancestors back as far as you have researched. There are various ways of preparing these family trees or pedigrees. If you have genealogical software then it will be able to do the work for you.

Regularly updating the family tree is also quite a good way of checking on your progress and ensuring you know who is related to whom.

One of the best ways of doing this is by using pedigree charts, sometimes called a birth brief, where you identify your direct ancestors. Direct ancestors are your parents, grand-parents, great-grandparents and so forth. The pedigree should start with yourself. There a few basic rules you should obey:

• Males always go above their spouses
• Females are always known by their maiden surnames
• You cannot show step-parents or other wives or husbands who are not your birth mother or father as they are not directly related to you by blood

The chart can help you work out what information you already have about your family and perhaps more importantly what you don't know. It can be amended and expanded as your knowledge grows. It is a good idea to date each draft, so you can measure your progress.

For the birth brief to be really useful, it should contain precise names, dates, places and occupations where known. All names should be recorded in full for each individual ancestor, as it is often not obvious what the surname was. Only those ancestors for whom there is documentary proof should be included.

As well as genealogical software there are various free templates you can download, such as those at www.pharostutors.com/freegenealogyhelp. php#downcharts.

Naturally the birth brief should be legible. You may want initially to write it up in pencil and ink in details when they definitely can be proved. High quality and attractive family trees and pedigree charts which you can complete yourself are available from Maxbal www.maxbal.co.uk or Family Tree Printing www.familytreeprinting.co.uk.

Ancestral Chart

Chart No. _____

No. 1 on this chart is
the same person as No. _____
On Chart No. _____

BORN
PLACE
MARRIED
PLACE
DIED
PLACE

NAME OF SPOUSE

BORN
PLACE
MARRIED
PLACE
DIED
PLACE

BORN
PLACE
DIED
PLACE

BORN
PLACE
MARRIED
PLACE
DIED
PLACE

BORN
PLACE
MARRIED
PLACE
DIED
PLACE

BORN
PLACE
DIED
PLACE

CONT. ON CHART _____

CONT. ON CHART _____

CONT. ON CHART _____

CONT. ON CHART _____

CONT. ON CHART _____

CONT. ON CHART _____

CONT. ON CHART _____

CONT. ON CHART _____

Form # F120

http://www.ancestry.com/save/charts/ancchart.htm

© 2007 The Generations Network, Inc.

Appendix VI

SOME PROBLEMS SOLVED ...

1. I have come across in a birth register two babies with the same forenames who were christened at the same time.
Is there anything which differentiates between them, such as parents' or siblings' names? But you may need to trace both lines until it becomes clear which one is 'your' ancestor.

2. The record, doesn't survive or the entry is missing.
The National Register of Archives (www.nationalarchives.gov.uk/nra) or Access to Archives (www.nationalarchives.gov.uk/a2a) databases may be able to help. They are unlikely to mention an individual ancestor, but may suggest alternative sources to be found at local record offices. There may also be other records with similar information. For example if you can't find a birth certificate, there might be records of a baptism in a church or an entry in a parish magazine.

The name may be spelt differently. Try all variations that you can think off.

The national indexes to births, marriages and deaths are full of errors. If you know where the event took place try the local registrar as their records are likely to be more accurate.

3. He just appears. How can I find where he came from?
You probably can't, especially if he turns up in London, but:

- He may have walked from a neighbouring village or along the main road going through the town.
- You may be able to pick him up on the IGI or 1881 census surname index by searching county by county – but remember there may be several people with exactly the same name.
- If he has an unusual surname it may only be found in certain areas of the country

4. She came from overseas, but I don't know where
Between 1851 and 1911 the country of birth (and occasionally place) is given in the census.

The place of origin is given in denization and naturalisation records and on alien registration cards. However, people who came from the British

Empire were already British citizens. And in any case many people did not seek naturalisation because of the expense (and few cards survive).

Ancestry.co.uk has several sources which may help: including incoming passenger lists (1878-1960) for ships arriving from ports outside Europe and a collection of early nineteenth century passenger lists and related records for people arriving from Europe.

5. He came from Ireland – how can I find out where?
With great difficulty. Irish men and women have never needed a passport to cross the Irish Sea. A family story or census entry might give a clue as to county of origin. Also useful is www.movinghere.org.uk

6. She's got to be in this document somewhere...
Is there a name index?

Victorian clerks often only entered names in registers by initial letter only, so you may to have to search all the names under the heading.

Don't stop at the first likely entry, she may turn up a page or two further on.

Remember variations in spelling of surnames, which often resulted from the clerk noting it down wrongly.

If all else fails ask the staff.

7. Her age is wrong?
Ages especially on census and death certificates are often a year or two out, as the individual may not have known his exact date of birth.

8. I can't understand the document
Whether it is hard to read or doesn't make sense – ask the staff for assistance or there may be an online help page which can help.

Somebody's bound to have had the same problem, so there may be a mailing list which may provide an answer. They are all listed at www.genuki.org.uk.

9. It can't be so...
You may have the wrong person – or you may have been making assumptions which are wrong – ie as to livelihood, size of family, marriage partner.

10. Well, I've tried everything, what can you suggest
Give up – the further back you, the harder it becomes. If you've tried all the reasonable searches - then you've done your best. Indeed you may find by researching somebody else or another branch the solution may suddenly come to mind. And I've found that some ancestors don't seem to want to be uncovered!

Appendix VII

RESEARCHING THE RICH

Not all of our ancestors were poor by any means and the chances are that somewhere on our family tree is somebody who was half-way eminent. In my case Major General William Crozier, who was a much respected general in the First World War, is supposed to be a distant cousin.

If you do find that you have a historical celeb in your family it is fairly easy to find out about them. Unless indicated you may be able to get access to these sources online if you are a member of your local library. In addition it is worth checking out Wikipedia, as it includes a surprising number of biographies (http://en.wikipedia.org).

Who's Who Published annually lists virtually everybody of importance with details of career, hobbies etc.

Who was Who When a person dies their entry is put into *Who was Who*. This work is published every ten years and covers a decade of the twentieth century. The volume the individual is in depends on his or her date of death. Winston Churchill, for example, died in 1965 – his entry is in the volume for 1961–1970.

Oxford Dictionary of National Biography (Oxford DNB) consists of short biographies of some 56,000 famous (and infamous) people in British history, with more being added every year. Search by name or by keyword and for each entry there is a short bibliography so you can find out more about them.

The aristocracy: Peers, baronets, knights and the landed gentry are recorded in various editions of *Burke's* and *Debrett's*. Of special interest to the family historian is that the lineage of individuals (usually for long established peerages) is often included. The current editions can be viewed online for a fee see www.burkes-peerage.net and www.debretts.com. Although not updated recently www.baronage.co.uk has a number of articles on researching the nobility and debunking a few myths.

Heraldry is, frankly, a minefield. The important thing to remember that coats of arms are granted to individuals so the stalls or shops you sometimes see which will sell you 'the coat of arms' of the Fowlers or whomever are selling fakes. They may be pretty but the chances that there is a link to your family is very remote. The College of Arms in London, which is responsible for regulating the granting of arms in England, Wales and much of the Commonwealth, is probably the best place to start: www.college-of-arms.gov.uk. Also of interest is the Heraldry Society (www.theheraldrysociety.com).

Appendix VIII

SOCIETY OF GENEALOGISTS

The Society of Genealogists is Britain's most important family history society. It was founded in 1911 as a place where professional genealogists and amateur enthusiasts could meet. Fortunately the stuffy atmosphere has long gone.

At its heart is the Library which is the largest specialist genealogical library outside North America. It has built up an unrivalled collection of material relating to family history. In particularly it has the largest collection of copies and transcripts of parish registers to be found anywhere. There are particular strengths in runs of genealogical and local history magazines, publications of local record societies and the histories of schools and colleges. And there are considerable archives mainly consisting of papers deposited by genealogists as a result of their searches. The catalogue is online. The library also provides access to the resources of the major online data providers without extra charge.

At a time when cataloguing of archive collections was limited members once devoted much of their time to indexing the records. The greatest of these indexes was Percival Boyd's Marriage Index compiled over a twenty year period which lists about an eighth of all marriages recorded in parish registers before 1837. Other projects include various series of wills, Great Western Railway shareholders and entrants to the Civil Service. Many indexes are now online either at British Origins (www.orgins.net) or through Findmypast (www.findmypast.co.uk).

Education has long been an important part of the Society's work with an academic journal *The Genealogist* for members. And there are two or three lectures or workshops a week, open to members and non-members alike, on all aspects of family history including courses for people new to the hobby, training on using genealogical software and tips for getting the best use from the internet.

Membership is currently £45 per year (£42 if you pay by direct debit). The Library is open to non-members for a fee of £4 per hour, £10 (4 hours), £18 (all day). Opening hours: Tuesday, Wednesday, Saturday 10am-6pm, Thursday 10am-8pm. Closed Monday, Friday and Sunday.

The Society of Genealogists, 14 Charterhouse Buildings, Goswell Road, London EC1M 7BA; tel 020 7251 8799; www.sog.org.uk

Appendix IV

SURNAMES

There are now some about 16,000 British surnames: most of which are only shared by just a few families. Before the thirteenth century people rarely had hereditary surnames: they were known just by a personal name or nickname. Surnames may have been spread by the need to identify individuals in legal documents, rather than by a nickname or physical description which varied during a man's lifetime. Most English families had adopted surnames by 1400, although surprisingly it wasn't until the eighteenth century that the practice became widespread in Wales.

The origins of surnames can divided into various categories:

- Place names (normally a town, village or even farm), such as Bristol or York
- Named after physical feature of place: Hall or Hill
- Derives from a nickname, perhaps derived from some physical character, such as Long, Short, Finch
- Relate to some family relationship, normally 'son of' (Richardson, Richards)
- Derive from an occupation: Smith, Archer
- Originate from a forename: Cutts (Cuthbert), Duncan, Gummer (Old Norse)
- Have arrived on these shores as the result of migration, from Ireland, Scotland, Europe or further field: Cameron, Milliband.

Sometimes names with different origins can merge into one, being similar in sound, but different in origin. The surname Blake may seem fairly straightforward but there are three quoted derivations. Firstly as a variation of *Black*, itself being a descriptive name; secondly originating as the old English word, *blac* meaning fair; and lastly being a corruption of *Ap Lake*, that is son of Lake in Wales.

Occasionally names can be assigned to an orphan or an immigrant. Foundling children for example might take the surname of the parish in which they were found, so if you find ancestors called John Cardiff or Sarah

Islington, for example, then it is just possible they were abandoned as babies. In the seventeenth and eighteenth centuries Africans in England were often given new names perhaps hinting at their exotic origin, such as Caesar and Strong.

Knowing the origins of a surname is unlikely to be of any practical use in your genealogy. The exception is those surnames that are very localised: Saggers, Sworder and Barnard for example are all largely found on the Hertfordshire/

Essex border. And the distinguished genealogist George Pelling discovered that his ancestors originally did come from Pelling, a small Sussex village.

Surnames change all the time, as new spellings are adopted either deliberately (Smythe for Smith), as the result of a bureaucratic error, or before 1750 because English spelling was still fluid. If, during your research, an ancestor appears to disappear one of the commonest reasons is that the surname changed, so it is worth checking common alternatives. I recently helped a John Gallagher try to find his First World War ancestors. John's grandfather spelt his name with a gh, but his father omitted the h (Gallager) and two generations before then it was Gallacker or sometimes Gallicker. And in Shakespeare's will, the playwright's name is spelt in three different ways – none of which was used in his lifetime or even today. So you've been warned!

Many family historians become interested in one particular name and try to trace all the holders of it. Many one-namers, as they are called, are members of the Guild of One-Name Studies. You can contact the Guild at www.one-names.org.uk or by post at Box G, Society of Genealogists, 14 Charterhouse Buildings, Goswell Rd, London EC1M 7BA.

There are numerous surname dictionaries, although to my mind none are really satisfactory. Undoubtedly, the most comprehensive is PH Reaney's *A Dictionary of English Surnames* (3rd edn. Routledge 1997) or Colin Rogers. *The Surname Detective* (Manchester University Press, 1995).

INDEX